# Journey to the White Rose in Germany

### By
### Ruth Bernadette Melon

Cover photograph by RB Melon and A. Collins: *Eye of the Lichthof*, Dome of
Ludwig-Maximilians-University, Munich, Germany 2003.

First published by Dog Ear Publishing
4010 W. 86th Street, Ste H
Indianapolis, IN 46268
www.dogearpublishing.net

ISBN: 1-59858-249-6
Library of Congress Control Number:    2006938633

This book is printed on acid-free paper.


Printed in the United States of America

# Author's Invitation

Decades after the White Rose leaflets appeared in Germany, 1942–43, distant memory, years of silence, cultural diversity, language barriers, and shifting boundaries, both political and emotional, have colored each account. In this re-telling, I am indebted to the published works of authors and translators who, in previous years, brought the narrative to the English-speaking world. The story is destined to be shared, to be passed along one to another, generation to generation. Translations of diaries, letters, and testimonies of eyewitnesses, including participants, relatives, and friends of the White Rose circle, have created the impulse and laid the foundation for continued study and discovery. Documentary video-material, including oral histories as well as the studies of Holocaust scholars, helped this volume present the milieu within which the White Rose grew.

Among the first to receive the leaflets of the White Rose were teachers the group hoped would spread the message of resistance. During my years as a middle school teacher, a student's reading first introduced me to Sophie Scholl. I needed to know more—thus my course was set.

Throughout my research and writing, I often pondered how easy it had been for me to duplicate lessons and distribute them to my students—to press a button on a machine that printed, collated, stapled, counted, and magnified whatever materials I had prepared for my classes—a matter of convenience. The machine's hum conjured images of White Rose handbills slipping off a hand-cranked duplicator hidden in secret places— a matter of courage.

Historians will continue their search for further clarification and amplification of the White Rose story; I am a link in the chain of teachers distributing the White Rose message as requested years ago. The story as I have studied and learned it, in my time and place in history, is told here in a manner that reconstructs and recreates dramatic moments supported by historic digressions and enhanced by reflections on its impact in the present. It is my best offering.

I have been encouraged by the words of Dr. Traute Lafrenz Page, a surviving member of the White Rose circle. In an evening phone conversation several years ago, she advised: If you want to know the White Rose, know the leaflets—study and analyze them.

The details of the personal lives of young German citizens like Alexander Schmorell, Christoph Probst, Hans Scholl, Sophie Scholl, Willi Graf, Traute Lafrenz, Franz Müller, Hans Leipelt and others, as well as teachers like Kurt Huber who dared to raise a voice against Hitler and his regime, may intrigue us. The events that unfolded during their lives and the culmination of their resistance may touch us deeply. But it is their messages left behind that provide the overarching, living truth of their story.

It has been my experience in re-telling and teaching this narrative, that lives are often changed: courage is instilled, reconciliation's doors are opened, and efforts for social justice are renewed. I invite you to travel to the White Rose in Germany. The journey is sure to impact your thinking and stir your spirit as it has mine. Please read the story and pass it on.

Ruth Bernadette Melon
At the home of
Victoria and John Scully
East Harwich, Massachusetts
July 2006

To my family
Past, Present, and Future

# TABLE OF CONTENTS

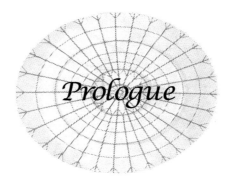

*Prologue*

## Teachers' Meeting
## Crailsheim, Germany
## August 11, 2003

"N OW," ANNOUNCED HERR HÜGELMAIER, "it is time to look at the picture." A massive oil painting by Gerhard Frank covered a vast expanse of wall in the foyer of the Geschwister-Scholl-Schule in Crailsheim. The jumbled conversation echoed around me as I stepped closer to absorb details that had escaped me when my computer's monitor first flashed the image months earlier. Then I sat spellbound at my writing table at home in the United States. Now I stood transfixed before the actual canvas with its re-creations of brick, steel, and concrete walls and towers—all tangled in chains and barbed wire— National Socialism in the Germany of 1933–1945. I could hardly believe my presence in the school was real.

Harry Nettlau, a recent high school graduate and son of the vice-principal, Ute Nettlau, acted as interpreter that August day. He raised his hands, directing attention to those artistic elements representing the concentration camps, the prisons— places that imperiled essential human freedoms. The shadows behind the barbed wire, Harry explained, are trying to make a connection with the outside.

The colors, shapes, and figures drew me even nearer. A crowd of faceless people bowed their heads, frozen and motionless; they were the bystanders. But opposite them, a faceless young man and young woman flung leaflets toward the crowd, sounding an alarm and heralding the possibility of saying, "No." The children of Geschwister-Scholl-Schule pass by a history lesson each time they brush up against Gerhard Frank's masterpiece. He has created for them a visual reminder of the siblings Hans and Sophie Scholl who, with a group of friends, mostly university students, voiced resistance to National Socialism in 1942–43. With Alexander Schmorell, Christoph Probst, Willi Graf, and the support of Professor Kurt Huber, as well as a small network of like-minded youths, they issued a call to passively resist the Third Reich's terrors: Wake up and think for yourselves. History would come to know them and their messages as the White Rose, the name given to the first four handbills.

I could not have known that a book report about Sophie Scholl, submitted by one of my seventh grade American students in the 1980's, would initiate a journey, both academic and personal. Not only would I learn of the youths' common bond of opposition, but I would also discover that it was first their love of learning, especially literature, the fine arts, philosophy, and theology, that brought them together in reading circles. There, ideas forbidden by the Third Reich could be explored and integrated by their developing intellects. As a humanities teacher with a strong interdisciplinary impulse, I did not find it strange that the seeds of justice and a growing concern for basic human rights germinated in soil that sets free the soul, disciplines the mind, and promotes creativity. Indeed, I wanted to know more, to investigate the "moral compass" that came to guide and motivate these young men and women.

Some educators emptying their mailboxes in the summer of 1942 were among the first recipients of several White Rose leaflets. The students hoped that teachers who had access to large audiences could awaken opposition to Hitler's regime.

The postscript on the first leaflets read: Please duplicate and distribute. Perhaps in teaching about the Holocaust in the 1980's, the stories of resisters seemed to be a frontier needing in-depth exploration as we developed our curricula. Then again, my own memories may have begged for such a narrative. Maybe it was the memory of a boy in my class who wore a ring strongly resembling the eagle and runic symbols commonly associated with the Hitler Youth, a ring given to him by his grandfather. This boy with the German surname remained silent and tense during class discussions about that dark time in the world's history. Or maybe it was the memory of a blonde-haired, blue-eyed eighth grader who told me her grandmother had been a secretary for the Nazis in France. Or perhaps it was the faint strains of an anti-Semitic German phrase I had learned as a child. We needed a narrative of the "other Germany."

In my American classroom the internal turmoil triggered during the years of the Third Reich still breathed. In the rows before me a third generation, mere children, awakened to the struggle for reconciliation among human beings. How was I to lead students to the consciousness of history's harsh realities without inviting reverse discrimination or stereotypes? The White Rose's call to teachers: Please duplicate and distribute, seemed to steer me in the right direction.

Pointing to fissures and fractures carved into the concrete fortresses' foundations and towers, Harry said: Look at the cracks in the walls. Totalitarianism is and was vulnerable. The artist's genius renders its final impact as the leaflets spill from the Scholls' hands over the edge of the mural's boundaries, onto wall, and over the floor. Past meets present. I reached down to touch the paper; the urge to pick up the leaflet embedded at my feet was too great. I wonder how many young boys and girls in this school have done the same.

The journey to the White Rose in Germany had begun several years before this August day in 2003. During a sabbatical year in 2001–2002, I completed a manuscript about the White Rose as part of a requirement for a Masters in creative nonfiction writing. During that time, I discovered several websites of German schools named for various individuals associated with the White Rose. Hans and Sophie Scholl's father had defiantly proclaimed that history would honor and remember his children. I thought it would be wonderful and revealing to visit some of these schools and discover how the story is taught, how the person is honored, and if the spirit of the White Rose lives there. The thought promised to materialize as the Geraldine R. Dodge Foundation granted me and three colleagues a fellowship for a ten-day trip to Germany to visit the Geschwister-Scholl-Schule and to network with teachers from the Christoph-Probst-Gymnasium near Munich.

Our first contact with one of these schools had come in May with an early morning international call to the Geschwister-Scholl-Schule's vice-principal, Ute Nettlau. For the boys and girls on the other side of the Atlantic, the school day had ended. We needed to time the call just right; our day in the USA had just begun with students joining in as the Pledge of Allegiance filtered through classrooms and corridors.

School hallways have always fascinated me; they are the places in-between where energy moves, where students and teachers make transitions, not only from one classroom to the next, but upon occasion, from one point of view to another. They are the connective tissue of the school community where secrets are shared, sins confessed, emotions released, and messages delivered. The corridors of Geschwister-Scholl-Schule may have been empty and quiet—its 300 children scattered for their summer vacation, some in rural villages and others in larger towns—but traces of the first through sixth graders' presence remained. Passing by a memorial plaque adorned with a white rose and portraits of Hans and Sophie Scholl, it was not difficult to imagine the students celebrating the September birthday of Hans Scholl, a time when they remember the meaning of civil courage and the challenge to exercise it in their own young lives.

Moving through the hallway, Ute stopped us at a bulletin board to show a world map tacked in a prominent position. Bold circles and colored lines connected Crailsheim-Ingersheim with places like Poland, England, Mongolia, Turkey, Italy, Kazakhstan, Spain, Portugal, Iraq, France, and other origin countries of various student body members. Many students at the Geschwister-Scholl-Schule have dual cultural identities, and Ute commented that immigrant students experienced varying degrees of adjustment to their adopted country as families responded to new demands. She insists students use the German language in school, but respects their abilities and use of their native language at home. Diversity is recognized and celebrated; strategies for conflict resolution help students formulate solutions for interpersonal problems—the antithesis of the homogeneity demanded by Hitler's regime more than sixty years ago.

Having made our passage from the lobby, we followed Herr Hügelmaier to the faculty room where we settled around a large table inviting us to quench our thirst with bottled water and juices and renew our energies with braided pretzels and croissants. The room's picture windows opened wide to trees shady but still, offering no relief from the summer heat wave. Birds twittered on some hidden branch, a familiar sound. Strangely, it felt like home, as if we gathered for a faculty committee meeting to discuss mission statements, realign goals, or propose new initiatives. But we had traveled thousands of miles from the USA for this teachers' meeting in Crailsheim.

I chose a chair at one end of the table, glad that Harry, our translator, sat next to me. To his left his mother Ute, also a sixth grade teacher besides being an administrator, had prepared tables laden with poster displays of materials, books, and photographs used for lessons about the White Rose, the Scholls, and the Third Reich. Next to Ute and at the other end of the table sat two musicians, separated by generations and language. At one corner was Ardith Collins, my young American colleague, a cellist and music teacher at our middle school in New Jersey. An experienced world traveler, the same age of the university students at the time of the White Rose, she eagerly accepted the challenges of this adventure. Next to her, Joachim Scharr, a retired German music teacher whose students at the Albert-Schweitzer-Gymnasium in Crailsheim had performed *Fiddler on the Roof* with a full orchestra in 1985, leaned forward to start a conversation. He lifted a pamphlet produced by a local organization, the *Arbeitskreis Weisse Rose,* explaining its purpose as documenting places and events important to the White Rose, the Scholls, and preservation of Jewish memorial sites. Herr Scharr contributes to the organization as an active member and leader. Manfred Hügelmaier, the principal, and our world language specialist, Bryon Pinajian, spoke intently in German. Bryon's history of world travel, his time living abroad, and his facility with the German language raised the comfort level of all present. Recording as well as participating, our educational technology specialist, Karen Orlando, worked her camcorder, documenting the events of our extraordinary day.

The room hummed with a camaraderie strengthening with each exchange. Herr Hügelmaier then focused our attention as he explained a school project: a calendar designed by the students and filled with photos and artwork depicting value-related themes supporting a school philosophy which encompasses responsibility for oneself, responsibility for the environment, and aid for the needy. He presented us with a gift calendar which would hang in our New Jersey classroom for years to come. Our students would later learn the German words for values like, peace, tolerance and friendship. They would see the efforts of students in a German White Rose school working toward these goals. We, in turn, presented our gift, a picture book illustrating Martin Luther King Jr.'s "I Have a Dream" speech. Along with his thank you, the principal remarked, "Martin Luther King Jr. is definitely a man who has to be remembered by people."

The tenor of the moment shifted. Hügelmaier answered an important question before I could ask, "Do you or how do you teach about the Holocaust in your German school?" This is a question many American teachers have entertained, and Hügelmaier, perhaps anticipating it, held up a book entitled <u>Judith and Lisa,</u> a picture story book written by Elisabeth Reuter, a resource used with the first through third graders. "Judith und Lisa waren die besten Freundinnen..." the story begins. With each page turned, the words and pictures relate the disenfranchisement of the Jews and the Third Reich's destruction of the relationship between Lisa and her Jewish friend, Judith. The young readers and listeners follow the story that tells of the man with the mustache who turns their lives upside down as storybooks by Jews are banned, and Jewish businesses are boycotted. Judith is ostracized at school and at play as German children fall prey to Hitler's propaganda of the superior race. Judith's father's pharmacy is destroyed on *Kristallnacht*, and blonde-haired, blue-eyed Lisa learns Judith will never return. One can imagine the questions and comments that might arise in an elementary school where one-third of the children were not born in Germany, where ethnic and religious differences are many, and where learning to live together is a basic principle. Frau Nettlau said each child is given a copy of the book to study the pictures and ponder the story.

I had hoped to discover if the White Rose's stand for basic human rights lived in the school named for the Scholls. As a member of the UNESCO Associated Schools Project, a network of schools committed to the ideals of human rights, democracy, and intercultural understanding, the Geschwister-Scholl-Schule not only re-membered the fragments of a painful past, but it labored daily to re-member the splintered humanity of the present, involving its students in activities like supporting water projects in Nepal and Tanzania.

Our tour of the school complete, Herr Hügelmaier said his goodbyes and sent us off to lunch and an exploration of Crailsheim-Ingersheim with the rest of the entourage. Leaving the school building, I turned once more for a final glance into the sunlit atrium where the leaflets proclaiming basic human rights would tumble from its walls for days and years to come. Across the narrow street, green hedges enclosed white-washed houses with steep red roofs. Trails of pink, red, and purple petunias cascaded from the balcony of a chocolate-colored A-frame. I took a deep satisfying breath but was caught short by the sound of a two-tone European siren snaking through the quaint neighborhood. The hi-low pitch to my American ears signaled images of danger, a sound familiar only from World War II movies and particularly the last scene of *The Diary of*

*Anne Frank*—the image of Gestapo wagons screeching to a halt on a street like this to drag some unsuspecting mother or father from home, leaving their child behind. The ghost vanished, and I felt some relief knowing that here, today, efforts continued daily to abandon no child, hide no history, and destroy no hope.

Following Ute, we headed toward the center of town where we met Ursula Scharr. Just a young girl in 1942, she would later have stories to tell. Our little group strolled through the platz where folks sought shelter from the sweltering sun in shady archways or beneath bright yellow umbrellas and purple awnings. Our hosts then escorted us to a Greek restaurant where we raised small glasses of ouzo in a salute of good wishes and good will. The bonds of our teaching profession somehow drew us closer than we had expected. In between bites of salad and sips of beer, the lively conversation continued. Moments of deep reflection now sprinkled with smiles and laughter. Ute admitted that years earlier as a young teacher she had her struggles. Like Sophie Scholl, she had engaged in her own inner conversations. "We have our past. Our generation after the war—we had to find our identity." She spoke of having to live with others' perceptions, "Oh—Oh—the bad Germans." Speaking of love of country and patriotism, she added, "I had a fear to show it. It took many years to come to normal thinking." Finally, she felt able to say, "I like my country."

I had brought another question with me to Crailsheim-Ingersheim, and Ute had answered it. How does a teacher in a White Rose school instill a feeling for democracy in her students? Did it relate in any way to the White Rose of the 1940's? Ute answered that learning democracy is living it. With great enthusiasm she described class sessions when she empowered her students through discussion, problem solving, and decision-making in the structure, activity, and management of their common learning. Their input, their opinions, and their thoughts held weight. The Scholls had grown up in a household supporting the idea that thoughts are free; the White Rose leaflets proposed to reclaim the right to think for oneself.

After thanking the proprietor for a delicious meal and

good service, the group once again set out to visit another White Rose site in Crailsheim, the house where the Scholl family had lived when Hans was born. At the edge of the landlord's farm, no marker or monument identified the house now rented by tenants not wanting the residence to become an easy target for extremist trouble-makers. Yet the *Arbeitskreis Weisse Rose* persists in its annual gathering there for a remembrance ceremony. Thinking of Robert and Magdalene Scholl as young parents, I stared at the windows and doorways, envisioning them there, a little family that could not have imagined the destiny that awaited them. Two cats sprawled out on the sidewalk in the afternoon's heat that began to weary us all.

It was then Ursula was ready to tell her story. With horror and passion she recalled events of the war that tore through her family and the town. We circled around her as she told how her sister who had Down's syndrome needed special protection for fear she would be swept up in Hitler's euthanasia disaster. Her father refused to send the girl to a home because he knew what would happen to his daughter. Ursula's bright blue eyes narrowed as she told how her father's name appeared on a hit-list of individuals uncooperative with the Reich. She held her face in her hands as she told how Crailsheim was destroyed when a very small band of Hitler Youths refused to accept defeat and tried to sabotage occupying forces. The result was a devastating Allied attack on Crailsheim, one that also destroyed the Jewish synagogue which somehow had survived *Kristallnacht* years earlier.

Our journey through town then brought us to the site of the Jewish temple, now a narrow street where the outline of the former synagogue walls is painted deep green on the pavement. Red geraniums and black-eyed Susans surround a small monument carved with a Star of David and a simple historical plaque that serves to remind those who would notice: Never Forget. Frau Scharr pointed to the words, "Love your neighbor." Harry told about a ceremony once held by the friends of the White Rose on *Kristallnacht* which they call the "Night of the Third Reich Pogroms." As he spoke, I imagined the pictures he presented. It was a dark November evening in this town of

33,000 people. Candles flickered one next to the other, illuminating the green outline of the destroyed synagogue. On the wall of a nearby building, a light show projected the images of some who resisted National Socialism. Music and poetry filled the street. Speeches preserved memories and warned of the dangers of Neo-Nazi extremist groups.

Then bells chimed four times, reminding us that our day in Crailsheim would soon come to an end. A final toast brought us to the *Konditerei* on the pedestrian mall where we gave the nod to German iced coffee. I expected shards of icy coolness to slip over my thirst, something similar to iced tea. What arrived was a tall glass filled with ice cream floating in a cool coffee soup topped with whipped cream. Our startled response amused our hosts; like most of our day, it was much more than we expected.

At the train station we took time for parting photos. Bryon asked, "What can we do for you?"

"Remember us," was Herr Scharr's simple answer.

I left with yet another question: Why had Gerhard Frank chosen to create faceless figures in the mural at the Geschwister-Scholl-Schule? I only had to search within to find the answer. Ultimately, I confront the question, "How would I have behaved if I had received a White Rose leaflet in my mailbox in the summer of 1942 or in February of 1943? Ignored it? Destroyed it? Turned it in to the Gestapo? Or would I have used it as a template for believing in and working toward a just society? Where would my face have appeared on the canvas?"

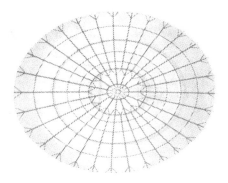

# MUNICH 1943

HANS AND SOPHIE SCHOLL STEPPED OUT from their rooms at Franz-Josef-Strasse 13 and slipped along the pathway from the hidden Garden House to Schwabing's busy streets. Left behind, a typewriter and an address book rested on Sophie's desk. Little appeared unusual about the pair dashing towards the university on this unseasonably warm morning in February. They blended easily with other youths in the students' and artists' quarter of Munich. One of them carried a suitcase; the other a leather briefcase. They hoped to go unnoticed.

There were many like Hans in the Führer's Wehrmacht: thick, wavy, dark hair, tall, trim, and handsome. Yet his searching, probing, intelligent eyes gave him a distinguished appearance. Within, a restless tension propelled him toward his destination.

Sophie, his sister, had just spent ten days at their family's Ulm home. Mother had been ill. Now she returned to resume her studies and other pressing business. Two days earlier she had written to her fiancé Fritz sharing her amazement with the transformation she felt when traveling the 150 kilometers from Ulm to Munich. She told him it was as if she left her hometown as a child and arrived at the bustling Munich bahnhof a confident young adult. Twenty-one-year-old Sophie did not have the Nordic, blue-eyed blonde look of the Führer's Aryan models but wore the face of southern Germany—dark hair, deep, dark eyes. Since she began her study of biology and philosophy at the university last May, she had drawn closer to her charismatic older brother. Today their purpose united them.

Suspicion permeated Munich like a heavy fog. In almost any German neighborhood in 1943, there lived a Nazi *Blockwart* who spied on the comings and goings of its residents and reported any peculiarities to the authorities. Very few Volk could predict who might be lurking in the shadows, waiting to pounce on an illicit word or action. Munich had given birth to the Third Reich. Here a *"Guten Tag"* needed to be whispered but a *"Heil Hitler"* shouted.

The brother and sister wove through the Schwabing neighborhood dotted with wine houses, artists' studios, and tiny apartments where students carved out study niches and gathered with friends for late night parties, even under threats of an air raid. Then it was straightway down Ludwigstrasse. This Thursday morning, timing was all important for the special delivery.

At the eastern edge of the city, the River Isar flowed past the Angel of Peace monument.

It was about 10:45 AM when the Scholls neared the Ludwig-Maximilians- University. The packed bags were heavy, but the students tried to appear nonchalant. One could never know what was going to happen next. Sophie had admitted to Fritz that she struggled with the unpredictability of each day. It depressed her. Dreams of the future and plans for happy occasions sometimes seemed futile, but she fought the shadows.

Recently, an incident at the university jolted the administration. A student-soldier had arrived for a philosophy class as usual, but the professor never appeared for the lecture. Some class members suspected trouble. Maybe authorities forbade him to teach; that sometimes happened if the instructor's veiled criticism of the Reich proved too transparent. Once again, when the students assembled for the next scheduled class, the professor did not attend. When the administration failed to answer students' inquiries concerning his whereabouts, fifty or so marched down Munich streets singing and finally stopping by the teacher's apartment to show him their support. Such oppositional behavior and demonstrations agitated school officials; Nazi policy held firm as university policy. Munich's nerves rattled in February 1943. Graffiti plastering "Down with Hitler" loomed large on campus and city buildings. A determined Gestapo scoured the university neighborhood.

Rows of students crammed the lecture halls of the stately campus building on the long, treeless Ludwigstrasse. Like Hans, many uniformed young men attending classes lived as half-soldier, half-student assigned to the Wehrmacht's student companies. At this hour, another philosophy professor, Kurt Huber, conducted a morning class. The school deeply entrenched itself in the Third Reich's ideology, and though Huber may have had loose ties to the National Socialist Party, he held some strong reservations, namely, Adolf Hitler. The teacher willingly risked the nurture of students' critical thought, something he had not sacrificed himself. Few seats remained unoccupied for his lessons.

Sophie and Hans could now see the doors leading to the university's atrium. Everything must be in place before the crowds poured out of the classrooms. Then they spotted two friends, Traute and Willi, leaving the building. Surprised to see one another, the four students stopped briefly and exchanged a few words. Traute looked forward to her upcoming weekend visit to the Scholls' Ulm home. Then the two friends hurried to catch a streetcar to the psychiatry clinic in another part of town. Traute felt confused, and Willi felt uneasy. They had seen the suitcase.

Hans and Sophie carried the product of the night's dangerous and exhausting work, but they and a growing circle of friends had committed themselves to bring thought to action. In the beginning, Hans had kept the campaign at a distance from his sister. When she learned of it, however, she committed.

Light filtered through the eye of the glass-domed ceiling, illuminating the empty spaces of the cavernous atrium, filling its balconies, and casting shadows in its archways. On a clear day the eye turned blue and clouds floated across its lens, opening the *Lichthof* to the world outside. Hans and Sophie moved quietly over the tiled floors. Cautiously, they opened the suitcase. Pulling batches of paper from the valise and the briefcase, they placed leaflets along the hall's perimeter, on the stairways, and in the long sunlit corridors where students could easily find them. They kept on, strategically planting the words like landmines on a battlefield. Even as Hans swept across the hallway, leaving a white paper trail behind, the draft of another message lay folded in his pocket.

Then Sophie and Hans scrambled up to the balconies, stacking papers and breaking away before students began to emerge from the classrooms. It was just about eleven o'clock now; they raced down the stairs and rushed towards the exit. Outdoors the warm air gave the feeling of spring. Ready to disappear down Schwabing streets, they noticed a few overlooked leaflets in one case. Perhaps because paper was too precious or the effort too great to waste the message, impulse overtook them, and the brother and sister abruptly returned to the foyer, bounding up the staircase again. From the upper floor balustrade, Sophie tossed the remaining leaflets into the courtyard below. Words trembled and floated on air, begging students to oppose the Reich and to lead the German people toward an alternative European world order.

The words of protest, the call to resist the Führer and his regime, had once more been set free. As Hans and Sophie turned to flee the building for a second time, a figure approached, prompting an alarmed Sophie to dodge into a room where she hid a key in an upholstered bench. An escape appeared fruitless. The man closing in on them barked: You're under arrest. When the lecture hall doors opened, crowds of students streamed into the corridors. Some snatched up the leaflets and read them. Others turned away. The university locked down.

# Chapter One

# BLOOD BROTHERHOOD

## 1934

HERR SCHOLL'S CHALLENGE DRIFTED lightly through the consciousness of his fifteen-year-old son. He urged Hans to think. The teen-ager understood his father did not approve, but he had his reasons. When Hans and other teen-age boys dressed and prepared to leave their homes for a meeting of the Hitler Youth, their schoolboy wardrobes, the pressed trousers, the white shirts, and woolen sweaters lay abandoned in their rooms. Instead, the boys sported black shorts and brown shirts with a swastika boldly banded on the left sleeve. Hans had grown taller and from his broadening shoulders hung lanyards, emblems of status earned by proving himself a worthy German youth. Hans displayed national pride. When the door shut behind him, he dismissed his father's warnings.

Tension in the Scholl household in 1934 did not deter family debate. Herr Scholl, an independent thinker with pacifist leanings, refused membership in the Nazi Party. He wanted his children to aspire to a free and principled life. Hans believed

Adolf Hitler's promises to bring Germany honor, prosperity, and community. He, like many others, grabbed the invitation: Play together, work together, and sing together. You are the future of a great and powerful Germany. Love the Fatherland and celebrate it together with your comrades.

Sports, outdoor adventure, education, music, radio, and movies organized the will of German youth. Thousands of youngsters read the story of Herbert Norkus, a Hitler Youth, who died at the hands of communist thugs as he was distributing National Socialist Party campaign leaflets. Tens of thousands thronged to the movie memorializing him, *Hitler Youth Quex*. On a panoramic screen they watched a youth turn from his parents, turn from carousing and listlessness, turn from his individuality, and turn to communal life in a Nazi dormitory. Norkus becomes a Boy of the Volk who in a final heroic act sacrifices his life for the New Order. Sights and sounds of honor and discipline captivated the audience.

Hans was not alone in his enthusiasm for Hitler's talk of unity, the Volk, and a brighter future for the German state. By 1934 his younger brother Werner and his sisters Inge, Sophie, and Elizabeth allied themselves with the Hitler Youth movement. Once Inge, the eldest Scholl, had vouched for her pure German ancestry free from any Jewish heritage, the *Bunde Deutscher Mädel* (BDM) welcomed her participation. In time, the BDM, the League of German Girls 14–18 years of age, counted her among its most prominent members in Ulm. It would not have been uncommon for admiring girls to greet her on the street. Younger braided girls with scrubbed faces smiled like the German poster girl and touted the motto: *"Be Faithful, Be Pure, Be German."* Crowds of teenagers dressed in BDM uniform white shirts and blue skirts would look to Inge as a role model, for she had proven herself efficient, dedicated, and popular.

Still, Robert Scholl warned his children not to trust Hitler. His persistent cautions met with stubborn retorts.

The young Scholls protested. They marveled at the Führer's leadership in technological advances like the autobahn.

Robert raised questions: What is the reason for the extra-ordinary investment of German muscle and expertise in a road project? Why have faith in Hitler's policies? Is it not possible there is a covert military purpose for the autobahn, namely the easy transport of troops and panzers? Robert would more likely support the development of industries of peace but not industries of war. His own experience with the military had been limited to the role of a medic during the Great War.

Robert's uneasiness may have grown as his children ventured forth to the parades on the streets of Ulm, gaining them a reputation for their rigor and hard-line involvement. His best logic could not compete with the emotional enticements that intoxicated his sons and daughters. He did not forbid their membership, hoping they would exercise reason.

Father did not withhold his own thoughts: Examine the remedies Hitler employed to improve the standard of living in Germany. Do not be misled by the homeland's rise from the rubble of an economic depression. Was it not a military buildup that energized the economy? Robert made his position clear: Corrupt leadership preyed on a German populace too ready to believe its lies.

Previous generations of Germans had their own conflicts with elders. Youths at the turn of the century had struggled against the restrictions of an imperial Germany that bound them to the ideal of obedience and submission. A formal and rigid society organized a caste of nobility, middle class, and workers, but boys and girls found ways to loosen the grip that frustrated their self-identity.

During Robert's youth, students of the German *Wander-vogel* stuffed their backpacks, hiked to the riverbanks, and climbed the jagged limestone of the Bavarian Alps. Retreating from the cities, they set up camp far from the authority of parents, the rigors of school, and the upper middle-class lifestyle. The wandering German youths created a counterculture trekking through the hills for long summer excursions into the forests and valleys where Germanic tribes had migrated and settled centuries earlier. They set out on foot, sometimes clad in bizarre-looking costumes that became their distinct signature.

A group might observe a certain prohibition such as abstinence from smoking or drinking or might allow a particular freedom such as nudism. Whatever the style or preference, self-determination ruled. By 1913, the wildly popular *Wandervogel* tradition assembled thousands of youth at the *Hohe Meissner*, a mountain peak wrapped in German legend. There teenagers celebrated fellowship with a festival of food, music, and rousing speeches.

But the Great War changed all that as wanderers became warriors and as the youth groups politicized. Fragments of the *Wandervogel* tradition scattered along the spectrum from left to far right. The Weimar government's attempts to suppress the newly emerging Hitler Youth group by declaring it illegal, created the opposite effect. The Nazi campaign to win over German youth went underground, and the forbidden became the attractive. Thousands of youths became the target of passionate Nazi propaganda.

The Nazi party staged its first massive Reich Youth Rally on October 2 and 3, 1932, three and a half months before Hitler became the Chancellor of Germany. One hundred thousand youths marched on foot or boarded trains to Potsdam. Over mountains, through forests, and across fields, bands of youths traveled, hailed as living proof that National Socialism could unify Prussia, Bavaria, Saxony, and Württemberg into one German society. Political opponents, however, intimated that behind the extravaganza's masque, children as young as six years old huddled hungry and shivering in drafty tents while party bigwigs lavished in the comfort and warmth of hotel rooms.

Robert Scholl reminded his children of the German legend of the Pied Piper of Hamelin and warned that the Führer cult would similarly entrap German youth. The Pied Piper narrative tells the tale of a German town plagued by a mass of rats lured to the river by the magical music of the Piper; there, in the Weser, the evil rats are drowned. The Piper comes to collect the price for his service and the town refuses to pay. The children of Hamelin hear the piper's sweet music, as the rats had, and now they abandon their mothers in the kitchen and turn their backs on their fathers' homes.

Pomp and circumstance thrilled the Scholl youngsters. Led by proud standard-bearers with banners unfurled over their heads, boys and girls marching in rhythm and outfitted in clean-pressed uniforms packed the sunlit city avenues. Precision demonstrated uniformity of action, thought, and desire. The standard-bearers, their right arms stiff and straight at the side, left arms crossing over heart, clutched wooden poles from which the swastika boldly hung. Thousands passed the review stand where the saluting Hitler acknowledged and affirmed them. Music, oratory, and pageantry pulled them into the whirlpool.

Hans' sister, twelve-year-old Sophie, was a member of the *Jungmädel*, the group for the ten to fourteen-year-old girls. Pro-German idealism drew many girls into membership that trained obedience, self-sacrifice, and loyalty to Nazi ideology. Both the *Jungmädel* and The Nazi League of German Girls, the *Bund Deutscher Mädel*, appealed to young girls with a poster showing a youth fit and firm reaching one arm skyward in a pose of grace and strength. Her slim yet muscular legs leaped across a clear blue sky that displayed the flowing folds of a Nazi banner bearing a prominent black swastika. When the Reich lifted the ban on female participation in athletics, girls hurried to compete at public sporting events. These freedoms cloaked the true Nazi purpose—social control of females and preparation as culture-bearers for the Führer.

Fervor for homeland and the adventure of outdoor hikes appealed to Sophie, reared in the countryside woodlands before moving to Ulm. For seven years her father had been mayor of Forschtenberg in the Kocher River Valley surrounded by vineyards and dense forests of beeches and fir. In the vintner's valley, Sophie's intimate connection with nature began to root. She did not resist the mountaineering, camping trips and bonfires with the girls of the *Jungmädel* but embraced the movement and recruited others. She progressed from member to leader, first for a small group of pre-teenagers, until her status at sixteen years old put her in the vanguard of larger groups of girls.

For the youth of National Socialism the outdoors was not

for meditation and solitary explorations, a setting for self-discovery; it was a place where children were taken away from their families. The regime enticed the children with skiing, swimming, horseback riding, and other activities that gave the illusion of freedom. Organized excursions away from the cities brought them to the countryside where white tents neatly lined lakes or riverbanks, and campfires lit night skies. No distinction separated the child who lived in the slums from the child who lived in a villa at the edge of the city. The nocturnal bonfire indoctrinated all in the spirit of the Volk.

National Socialism may have promoted a way of life contrary to self-determination, but Herr and Frau Scholl maintained a humanistic attitude. Inge Scholl remembered her father's assurance that they were entitled to their opinions—the right to form their own beliefs. In Robert and Magdalene's home, books had encouraged the children to think imaginatively. The works of artists, philosophers, and literary figures, mirroring individual creative potential, found their place on bookshelves. Magdalene, having served with an order of Protestant sisters at a Red Cross hospital during WWI, cherished the Bible as a centerpiece of that collection.

When she was a little girl, Sophie often turned the pages of a favorite book, *When the Root Children Wake Up*. The imaginative and colorful tale narrated the secret hidden activities of children living underground who bring life back to the earth's surface after a long, barren winter. The children restore vibrancy and life to the colorless world. Now Robert Scholl tried to awaken his own children, telling them that they too had slept long enough. Sophie could not have known this story might prove a template for a life's purpose.

On New Year's Day 1934, thousands gathered around radios in family living rooms to hear Baldur von Schirach, the Reich leader of the Hitler Youth, appeal for unification of the nation's young. His commanding voice skyrocketed him to power and prestige; his passionate and dramatic addresses to the youths transformed him into a mythic celebrity. Turning up the volume, the young audience heard messages urging them to submit their wills to the Führer, following him to the gates of hell if required. Schirach hailed the new year as the beginning of fearless dedication to a blood brotherhood in which comradeship was all, and the flag meant everything.

The campaign's magnetism pulled Hans closer and closer to its center. When twenty-six-year-old Schirach appeared as the *Reichsjugentführer* of the Hitler Youth, he epitomized the Reich's ideal of youth leading youth. A role model and a graduate of the University of Munich, he wielded tremendous influence, convincing youngsters that they represented the spearhead of a thousand-year era of National Socialism. He assured them that future generations would benefit from their hard work and sacrifices.

Many Hitler Youths did not enjoy the educational and economic advantages of Hans and his siblings. Though Robert Scholl had encountered his own employment and financial difficulties, support for his family improved over time. Many believed the Führer showed generosity when he rescued children from the squalor of the cities, transplanting them to the country to feed, clothe, and house them in the fresh alpine mountains. Schirach's strategies for recruitment reached directly to the needs and wants of families paralyzed by economic depression.

Hans' outgoing personality and charisma proved excellent leadership material. Physically fit and handsome, he marched ahead within the ranks of the youth movement. He loved southern Germany's landscapes. The rigorous hikes and adventurous camping trips tempted boys who sang in the darkness as stars replaced the last colors of the evening sky. Logs arranged in a glowing tripod flamed into the black night. Brown Shirts sat with arms clasped about their legs, some resting their heads upon their knees as they sang melodies that stirred them with the feeling of camaraderie. Faces reflected the light of the bonfire igniting a spirit that bound them to each other. During a summer solstice ceremony, youth members solemnly lit their torches from the flames of the SS. As smoke billowed from the blaze, the independent, non-political spirit of the old *bundische* tradition dissipated. Schirach and the Hitler Youth doused any embers of that youth movement popular during the Weimar Republic. It became more and more difficult to remain in the Hitler Youth organizations and maintain a free spirit. Yet Hans persisted, attempting dual loyalties despite the troubles.

Hans often accompanied his group with his guitar as they sang around the campfire. As he relaxed into the fraternity of the group, his repertoire began to expand to a number of international folk songs.

Discord interrupted: Un-German folk songs, he was admonished by a superior, were not to be sung, not to be performed. Hans found it unthinkable that the minor modes, the color and mystery of the fascinating Russian rhythms were now *verboten*. Uncertainty began to ruffle his confidence, but he tolerated the contradictions, content to remain within the group.

At seventeen years old, Hans' status rose to *Fähnlein-führer*, a troop leader empowered to order boys about and to expect obedience without question. He could supervise as many as one hundred and fifty younger boys. The Reich awarded the Dagger of Honor to achievers like Hans, an acknowledgment akin to a rite of passage into manhood, when a boy becomes a full member of the community. Rank and ceremony inflated adolescent egos.

As the solemn ritual began, a youth would step forward from the group. With arms held stiffly at his side, shoulders drawn back in attention, his eyes focused on the impressive officer opposite him who proclaimed the presentation of the weapon. The boy heard a voice assure him that God had given him comrades who were there for him if he should fall, as he would be there for others.

Commitment to comradeship had its rewards.

The Führer cultivated a future army with obedience as the natural order. During field exercises, young boys rolled through tall golden grasses, tumbling down slopes in hand-to-hand combat. The piercing shriek of the whistle blew, and bands of boys charged each other in mock warfare, locking each other in the grip of battle. Towheads grabbed at knees and necks, pulling at arms and pouncing upon each other, hoping to be named victors in the combat games. In the school of violence, strength overcame hurt and pain.

*"Praise Be to What Makes You Hard."* Drills turned to incidents as the Brown Shirts warred with Catholic youths in streets and alleyways. The right worldview of superior and inferior dominated the Hitler Youths' ideological lessons of purity of race, lessons carried out during mid-week home meetings. Hans remained rooted in its center.

In 1936 the Hitler Youth selected Hans Scholl as standard-bearer for his regional troop at the Great Party Rally in Nuremberg. The day was bright; the Zeppelin Field filled with columns of youth uniformed and arranged in geometric patterns across the arena. Thousands more packed the bleachers surrounding the parade below. The spectacle in the arena obliterated class distinction; individuality blurred in the unfolding drama. An occasional onlooker with outstretched arms raised a camera overhead and aimed the lens in the direction of the Führer, hoping to catch him on film. Thousands of banners pointed skyward. Tens of thousands of boots tapped in unison. Waves of children and teenagers proudly marched in review before Adolf Hitler.

*"One State, One People, One Leader."*

Drummers waited their cue while the crowds raised their fists, punching the air. Communal song reverberated throughout the field. Little children clapped their hands in delight. The throng pledged its oath of allegiance to Hitler, and the thrill of the demonstration excited the small bands of youths from across Germany. They were young, strong, and destined for a promising future in a New Germany.

Eighteen-year-old Hans Fritz Scholl was one of them.

But for Hans, at Nuremberg, something went terribly wrong. He felt drained from the incessant marching, singing, and euphoria. Perpetual motion sabotaged thought. Near exhaustion, he returned home to Ulm subdued and pensive.

Hans withdrew into an uncharacteristic silence. His sisters noticed. Curious, but willing to allow their brother his brooding space, they did not approach him. They simply understood a significant change had occurred.

The rally left him with uneasy feelings about the direction of the youth movement. Everyone dressed alike, sang the prescribed songs, marched in step, and chanted the party slogans. The narrow regimentation of the thousands in the crowd suddenly struck Hans as having little concern for the individuality of those assembled. Their ideas and opinions counted for nothing. The repression of thought shook him and collided with his search for self.

The uniqueness of each German boy dissolved in the mass. Hans began a slow retreat from a Führer cult that insisted on absolute concession to its worldview. Neither could his brother Werner shake off the values of the old *bundische* traditions now outlawed by the Reich.

The Scholl sisters watched.

After the tremors at Nuremberg, a series of emotional aftershocks struck Hans, attacking at a critical stage in the formation of his self-identity. An emerging awareness began to change his perception of National Socialism's purposes. He believed each boy under his command had a contribution to make to the little society they created. He believed in their right to self-expression. Together they designed a contingent pennant bearing the figure of a mythological beast, which they would carry when their platoon marched in rallies and other public events.

On one occasion, Hans' boys fell proudly into formation, ready to march, ready to move eyes right, eyes left, eyes forward and ready to obey the commands as they were called. A young Brown Shirt under Hans' tutelage stood at attention for the compulsory inspection of the troop. Filled with pride, he held the group's banner aloft.

Suddenly, a strange harsh voice bellowed for the youth to lower the flag—to hand it over.

The boy hesitated.

The command repeated: Give it up. Only regulation symbols are worthy in a rally of Hitler Youth.

The boy stood frozen, refusing to release the handiwork of his comrades.

Hans sprang into action in defense of the boy. Anger took hold of him. A threat to one of them was a threat to him. He moved out of the formation, charged forward, raised his arm, and slapped the commander.

Tears ran down the flustered face of Hans' young follower. Infuriated, the cadre leader clutched the confiscated flag in a tight fist. Hans would pay.

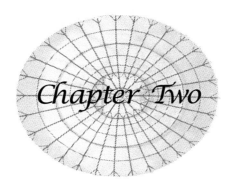

# Chapter Two

# SUBVERSION

THE GRUFF VOICE OF THE HITLER YOUTH leader demanded: What are you reading? Hans, now stripped of his status as a *Fähnleinführer*, identified the book's author as Stefan Zweig.

The voice fired: *Verboten.* Give it up.

Hans shot back: Why is this book banned?

Silence was the answer. But Hans knew the author was a Jew.

For Hans, this was another passionate voice that had been telling him stories since he was a child sitting cross-legged, his head buried in Stefan Zweig's book, *Sternstunden der Menschheit (The Tide of Fortune)*. The biographer had transported Hans as a witness to history crystallized in twelve lives illuminated by a moment of extraordinary insight, creativity, and adventure. Time and again Hans opened the collection and read through pages narrating George Frederick Handel's near-death and his triumphant spiritual journey through his illness. The author's poetic prose uncovered Handel's heart as the musician composed his great masterpiece, *Messiah*. Dramatic stories relating historic moments of enlightenment enthralled Hans. He treasured the Handel story and others like "Scott

Reaching the South Pole" or "Lenin Leaving Zurich." Zweig's book, a boyhood companion, accompanied Hans even into his Brown Shirt days.

*"Deutschland Erwache! Judah Verrecke!"* (Germany Awake! Judah Perish!) Slogans and prohibitions that threatened to erode his inquisitive mind, signaled danger. Hans balked at sacrificing a favorite book, unwilling to trash it because the author was a Jew and a pacifist. The Reich's propaganda began to lose its hypnotic effect as the boundaries set by the regime irritated his strong will.

But leaving the Hitler Youth meant setting oneself apart, not belonging, losing status. Hans chose to remain a member despite his misgivings, but soon he would seek companionship elsewhere.

Sophie, too, experienced cracks in her staunch support for the regime's youth movement. Earlier it had confused her when two Jewish girlfriends were not allowed to be members of the *Jungmädel*. She wondered why they were excluded when she was the dark-haired, dark-eyed girl with a deep complexion while one of her forbidden Jewish friends was blonde and blue-eyed.

Another time, Sophie's youth group compiled a booklist of titles to be shared at weekly meetings. Sophie, intelligent and well-read, suggested the works of Heinrich Heine, a poet greatly influenced in his early years by German Romanticism. True, he had turned to satirical works, some of which had been banned by the German authorities in the nineteenth century. True, he had left Germany to live, die, and be buried in Paris, but Sophie did not expect her suggestion to be rejected so vigorously. The response: No, there is no room for Heine here. Heinrich Heine was of Jewish ancestry, although he had converted to Protestantism. Sophie was not prepared to give away an author she considered a cornerstone of German literature. Slowly, she began to understand the wisdom of her father's objections, but several years would pass before she left the League of German Girls.

Hans and his brother Werner did not let the Reich's laws stop them from joining the dj.1.11, the German Boys League of the First of November, so named for its founding date. Even though he maintained his associations with Hitler Youth, Hans found in the alternative d.j.1.11, intellectual and artistic young men representing a last vestige of the *Bündische Jugend*, hearkening back to the old *Wandervogel* tradition. Frau Scholl welcomed the new group in her home, baking pastries and giving them the privacy they wanted for their gatherings. The boys' music, poetry, and literary pursuits did not go unnoticed by Sophie and her sisters, Inge and Elisabeth.

The Scholl boys renewed the tradition of youthful autonomy: hiking, camping, and skiing in the mountains with their new comrades. Hans reclaimed the freedom to sit beside a campfire with his companions singing folk songs from faraway places; no one in the dj.1.11 called it un-German. Now he had friends with whom he could have a thoughtful conversation, and whether it was about music or art, self-expression was valued, not forbidden. They exercised their freedom of choice with great risk. National Socialism had declared membership in this organization an illegal act.

The Gestapo combed the countryside, the towns, and cities searching for young criminals during 1937. Entering homes, uninvited and without a warrant, they were on the trail, tracking like bloodhounds, sniffing out evidence, and scratching at doors they suspected belonged to members of outlawed youth groups. Rummaging through personal possessions, invading private spaces, they picked their way through the lives of German citizens in search of youth involved in illicit groups. The sole legal youth organization in Germany was now the Hitler Youth. The goal was total classless unification.

The Gestapo pressed on, crumpling and shredding pages of diaries, personal creative writing, poetry, and essays in an effort to save National Socialism from the contamination of free thinking and its expression. State police cornered offenders and dragged them to prison. Hans, now nineteen, was suspect because of his association with the d.j.1.11. The Gestapo closed in just as he was beginning military training for the cavalry at Bad Cannstatt, fifty miles from Ulm.

The Scholl household did not escape the watchful eye of the Secret State Police. Two stern figures, framed in the doorway of the Scholls' home, demanded entry.

They arrived to round up the Scholl youths now under investigation for participation in subversive activities.

Tension mounted with the Gestapo's frightening invasion of their home. Hans was not in the house, but the others, guarded and cautious, gathered together. Shaken and straining to keep their wits about them, the parents, though alarmed, acted swiftly. Robert, an adept politician, occupied the investigators while his wife Magdalene evaded their scrutiny and managed to conceal evidence that could incriminate her sons.

But the Gestapo intended to arrest her children. They brushed Magdalene's vehement protest aside, and she watched in horror as the men carried her youngsters off to a local jail. Later, the authorities released Sophie, mistaking her for a boy, but detained Inge and Werner. Their destination: a detention center in Stuttgart, fifty miles northwest of Ulm.

Hazardous weather conditions made the transfer a harrowing journey for Inge and Werner. Gray clouds hovered over the city of Ulm as a winter storm swept into the region, quickly covering roads with drifts of snow. The brother and sister huddled in an open truck surrounded by others who had been taken into custody. The icy winds blasted the captives as the vehicle drove off to Stuttgart. Along the autobahn, the vehicle moved through perilous terrain taking them farther and farther away from home. At last they arrived at the Stuttgart prison, cold and frightened, where they were thrown into solitary cells.

A week passed before interrogations began. The Gestapo officers quizzed Inge about her knowledge of resistance groups and her opinions about resistance itself. When the authorities finally released Inge and Werner, a relieved Magdalene arrived in Stuttgart to accompany them home. They would not easily forget this encounter; the incident left its sting, especially wounding Sophie's sense of justice.

HANS WAS IN THE BARRACKS when the Gestapo arrived for him. He was in training to wear the Wehrmacht uniform and to ride the military steeds of an imposing cavalry. The new trousers to complete the military attire still needed tailoring in Stuttgart. Now, instead of sending his son cash to cover expenses, Robert Scholl sent letters to Hans' commanding officer, asking him to intervene. Could he take some action to protect Hans from the Gestapo?

Scupin, Hans' captain and squadron commander, liked the young Scholl and saw his leadership capabilities; he was able to forestall the Secret Police's interest in Hans for a short time. But the Gestapo snatched Hans from the ranks and carried him off to Stuttgart and a narrow prison cell. With Hans in custody, the authorities grilled him with questions about his "subversive activities" and his interactions with Hitler Youth boys formerly under his charge.

Days of detention turned into weeks. Herr Scholl and Scupin exchanged letters in an effort to secure an overdue release for Hans. Christmas 1937 approached, and Hans worried that his imprisonment would ruin the family's holiday festivities. He feared he had brought the Gestapo's attention to them, placing them under further surveillance. In the first days of his confinement, he admitted to despair. The season turned bleak, but the week before Christmas, Robert Scholl visited his son. Renewed by his father's concern and encouragement, optimism reawakened. Hardly a day had gone by since the meeting with his father when Hans wrote a note to his parents with fond reminiscences of his childhood, a happy and proud time. Thanking them for the strength they instilled, Hans pledged to do some good during his lifetime.

On Christmas Eve, *Rittmeister* Scupin entered the remand prison and discovered Hans housed with two other inmates. The captain did not like this arrangement and spoke with the judge to make adjustments. A member of the Wehrmacht, the captain argued, deserved respect. During this visit, Hans assured Scupin that the charges against him could not be upheld. Scupin argued again on the man's behalf, saying he would take responsibility for him and see that he returned to his training at the camp. Then the captain left the prison for a holiday. Hans remained alone in his cell on Christmas Day.

Later, after a bureaucratic tangle, the authorities freed Hans.

The snows of the New Year 1938 crunched beneath Hans' feet as he wearily alighted from the cab in the early morning hours. His release from prison did not close the case. It would be months before the celebration of Austria's annexation prompted a pardon from the government. For the moment, he needed to make his way through the snowdrifts to his bed in the barracks. In four hours he would report to the firing range.

During the months of basic training the letters to and from home arrived with regularity. The experience of mother, father, and home had taken on a new dimension after his struggles with the Gestapo. He wrote to his parents confessing his disgust for a crowd mentality that refused to question the war but remained enamored by heroism's mystique. Relationships, too, shifted shape as the teenager foundered along the way to adulthood.

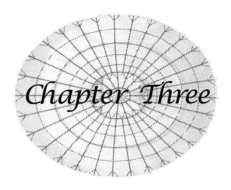

# Chapter Three

# SABOTEURS

WILLI GRAF STOOD FOR THE GOSPEL READING at Sunday Mass. Across the aisle and in pews throughout the church, other teenagers of the parish may also have offered quiet attention. Church-goers had to be careful, though. Upon occasion a youth might not attend for private devotion or communal celebration but rather as a spy for the Reich. Such young Nazi collaborators waited and listened for a homily that counseled parishioners against joining the Hitler Youth or warned parents of its negative influences. Such cautions could send a priest to prison.

When Sunday Mass at the Roman Catholic Church ended, Willi would often return to his family's home in Saarbrücken. If a teen-age junior Gestapo member had heard a pastor's remarks critical of the Nazi youths, he would hurry to report suspicions to his superiors. The juvenile police force waged war against Catholic youths, branding those who refused to join the Hitler Youth movement, "saboteurs of German unity."

From the time Willi was eleven years old, he resisted the propaganda and pressures to join the National Socialist youth organization. Like thousands of other Roman Catholic children in Germany, he had followed the *Wandervogel* tradition as a member of the *Neudeutschland*, a Catholic youth group for boys. There he learned to act independently and creatively while under the guardianship of a spiritual leader—a compromise to complete autonomy. The *Neudeutschland* boys devoted themselves to the traditional camping and wandering excursions while at the same time they nurtured the rituals, practices, and beliefs of German Catholics. Boys gathered together making the Sign of the Cross and sharing communal prayers.

With like-minded Catholic companions, Willi explored the surroundings of Saarbrücken. Instead of the HJ *(Hitler Jugend)* brown shirt, the boys wore the white shirt and gray trousers of the *Neudeutschland.* He and his friends wandered past the palaces, castles, and baroque houses of the Saarland, the frontier area between Germany and France formed by the river Saar. From a high point overlooking the town, the grounds of a nineteenth-century castle offered a fine view of the city with its lively district of St. Johann. Nearby stood St. John's Roman Catholic Church.

If their excursions took them farther north, following the winding course of the river, they might pass through a series of villages during the grape harvests of October, or during November when the yeast began to settle and the wine began to clear. Willi was a son of these borderlands where his father made a livelihood in the wholesale wine business, selling quality wines in the brown bottles of the Rhine region or the green bottles filled with Moselle and southern German wine. These were the same borderlands which the Treaty of Versailles had awarded to France, the territory west of the Rhine with coal fields and the provinces of Alsace and Lorraine. Here lived the Grafs, a Catholic Rhineland family, in a home where Willi sang his hymns and learned from his mother to offer help to the needy. When, in 1935, the Saarland became German again, Willi's father became a NSDAP member. Here Willi's father hosted National Socialist gatherings in the Johannishof festival hall, part of his business establishment.

Until 1933, some German clergy had discouraged

Catholic participation in the Nazi Party. Often they excluded party members from the long lines of communicants. The German Catholic Church prohibited it. In the early 1930's some Catholics did not join the Nazi Party because their pastors forbade it. In some parishes groups of Nazis did not attend Roman Catholic burials or other religious events. The priests banned it. German bishops had made declarations of the errors of National Socialism, and the Catholic Center Party stood as a threat to the power of Hitler's Nazism.

Fifteen-year-old Willi Graf enlisted in the Catholic campaign to contain Nazi contamination. In contrast to his father's attitudes, he struck names from an address book's list of friends, noting next to each "HJ" if they had buckled under to the Hitler Youth. He would no longer call upon them. Others may capitulate to the pressure and join the Führer's youth movement, but he would not.

The songs and pageantry of the Hitler Youth pervaded the German streets. Willi's Nordic appearance—the muscular breadth of his shoulders, his blonde hair and blue eyes—mirrored the images of young manhood in promotional posters for Hitler Youth recruits. In appearance he was a model Nazi; in his heart and soul he was not.

Willi was not the warrior daredevil praised by the lyrics in the Hitler Youth songbooks; he was a thinker—given to pondering, apt to brood over some philosophical question. The Nazis clung to emotion more than reason. The Hitler Youth nurtured instinctual behavior and discouraged intellectual pursuits. They considered boys like Willi, the product of an educated middle class, "intelligence beasts with paralysis of the spine." The songs and the messages that stirred Willi breathed from the Holy Scriptures. He loved Psalm 96 which he described as magnificent.

When Hitler became Chancellor in 1933, he knew that German Catholics had allegiance to another authority figure, the Pope in Rome. In order to achieve absolute power over the Volk, the Führer had to compete with Catholics' religious loyalties, and the Catholic Church knew Hitler's rise to power could diminish Papal claims of absolute authority. In July of

1933, just five months after Hitler became Chancellor, the Vatican reached a concordat with the Third Reich. A concordat was a type of agreement made by the Catholic Church in behalf of its members with governments in a particular country. It was the first bi-lateral agreement the new regime made with a powerful international organization, and for that reason some perceived it as the Church's acceptance of the Nazi regime. Others recognized it as an attempt to protect the threatened rights of Catholics under Nazi policies. Hitler did not want to risk the rejection of the Catholic Church which could potentially form an international coalition of resistance outside of Germany.

On behalf of Pope Pius XI, Italian Cardinal Eugene Pacelli, then Vatican secretary of state, negotiated the *Reichkonkordat* of 1933 between the powers of the Roman Catholic Church and the State in Germany. No clergy could remain in political parties or serve an official function in government. This concession distressed some German clerics, but the moderates prevailed.

In the weeks before the signing of the *Reichkonkordat*, Nazi fanatics had taken to the streets carrying out arrests of priests who were members of the Catholic Center Party or assaulting gatherings of Catholic youth groups. The Catholic Center Party was fated to self-dissolution thereby eliminating a potential threat to the Nazi Party.

Throughout the political upheaval and arguments surrounding vague language and interpretation of the various articles of the concordat, millions of German youth journeyed through adolescence seeking a path to adulthood. How were these agreements made by adults going to affect Willi's life? How would Willi's Catholic youth group, the *Neudeutschland*, adjust to agreements made between the Nazis and the Church?

Willi battled to preserve his loyalties as the street fights escalated in cities throughout Germany. He, too, had felt the sting of an insult and a knuckled fist. In Cologne, the Hitler Youths attacked Catholic youngsters gathered in front of churches. Three months later, the Vatican sent a greeting to its young congregants in Germany, praising them for their faithfulness to God and Church and instructing them that in doing so, they strengthened their faithfulness to their country. The words rallied those Catholic youths who labored to integrate their loyalties to God and loyalties to their country. Now they had been told by their spiritual leader that they honored Germany through preservation of traditional spiritual values and practices.

The most contentious article of the *Reichkonkordat*, Article 31, stated: Only those Catholic organizations that were religious, cultural, or charitable would be protected from interference from the Reich. Sporting activities and other state-sponsored youth activities would not be scheduled on Sundays to avoid conflicts with religious observances.

Even as the regime made concessions to the Catholic groups, an intense campaign grew to enroll all German children in the Hitler Youth. Hitler told Baldur von Schirach that he expected winning over the Catholic youth to be a very slow but ultimately a successful campaign. Schirach did not believe that the Catholic youth groups had the right to exist on their own, so he continued to exert pressure.

Hitler did not uphold his concordat agreements; his obsession was victory for his cause no matter how achieved. Within time, Willi's group lost the freedom to wander the countryside wearing the uniforms of the *Neudeutschland*. Church youth activities could occur only within the physical boundaries of Church property. Sports, sponsored by the Church, had to end. The state claimed exclusive rights to the physical education of all the German youth.

Willi and his friends, deprived of public displays of solidarity, could no longer march through the streets as a group. The Catholic world responded with imaginative solutions to the restrictions. Minor religious festivals became major ones giving the faithful a reason to assemble in large visible groups. Tens of thousands of Catholics began pilgrimages to cathedrals where they would hear sermons encouraging them to be fearless and loyal. Often they would recite pledges of loyalty to God, Rome, and Germany. Local fanatical Nazis demonstrated their own understanding of the *Reichkonkordat* as debates arose concerning what was in the arena of religion and what was in the arena of the state.

Even though the Papal agreement allowed the Catholic groups to exist, it failed to halt the Nazi campaign to win over boys like Willi. Truckloads of youths, raising the Hitler Youth flags and trumpeting their presence, cruised through towns in banner-wrapped vehicles proclaiming pro-Nazi slogans. The street war between the Hitler Youth and the Catholics continued as Nazis insinuated that Catholic boys were not good patriots. Some Catholic youths survived the pressure; others did not.

Hitler Youth security patrols victimized Catholic boys along city streets as brutal beatings and ambushes turned harassment to assault. Some Catholic youths tried to solve their dilemma by retaining dual membership in the Hitler Youth *and* the Catholic Youth organizations. At eighteen years old, some of Willi's peers, after graduating secondary school and giving the required work service, sought to make their way into the adult world through apprenticeships or jobs in German industry. The German Labor Front locked their doors in the face of those who were not members of the Hitler Youth. As a result, the ultimatum sounded: It is one or the other, not both. Thousands of Catholics conceded to the Hitler Youth. Economics won out.

Still, Catholics continued to make pilgrimages, even as far as Rome to the Holy See. Willi journeyed with his *Neudeutschland* group to make an Easter pilgrimage to the Vatican. At times Pius XI granted an audience to some German youth groups as he did for two hundred members of *Neudeutschland* and one hundred members of the youth of *Sturmschar* on April 3, 1934. The youngsters listened intently as he addressed them with words recognizing their courage and loyalty and urging them to "...always speak the truth, and defend the truth, and defend therewith your rights, which are the rights of conscience."

Churches throughout Germany posted Pius XI's message. The Church took the offensive for its youth, and Nazis responded with demonstrations and jeers, tearing copies of the message from church doors in an effort to silence the Pope's voice.

Willi Graf understood the importance of the rights of conscience. Even though he had grown up in a traditional Roman Catholic family, observing all its rituals and practices, he demanded of himself a thorough inner commitment based on a personal search for God. He accepted his spiritual inheritance but not without question.

During the Easter season in April of 1935, members of the *Neudeutschland* again made their way to Rome. On the return trip they marched unmolested past the Italian border guards. The boys continued their journey, reaching the Swiss patrol that let them pass undisturbed. When they reached the border of their own country, the German officials stopped the sixty buses and a group of over one thousand. Guards stockpiled the youths' knapsacks. They forced boys to surrender rosaries and prayer books. Mounds of cameras and musical instruments grew as the officers confiscated private property.

Not long after this incident, the Reich issued decrees further suppressing the Catholic youth activities. Police took the side of the Hitler Youth, often ignoring harassed Catholics. By the end of 1935, repressive action against the Catholic youths increased. Willi witnessed the emergence of the Hitler Youth Law of 1936 and its executive order issued in 1939 which obligated German youth to join the Reich's youth movement. The *Neudeutschland* dissolved.

Still, Willi would not yield.

He refused to follow Hitler blindly, but rather had already joined the *Grauer Orden,* an unauthorized, illegal Catholic youth group—young men who gathered together in a search for a personal philosophy based on spiritual values, theology, and church reform. The illicit organization found ways to organize in secret, even if it meant meeting on a steamboat on the Rhine River. It did not intend to crumble under the Nazi's pressure to conform.

In 1936 Willi posed for a photograph while on an excursion with his friends of the *Grauer Orden.* He sat atop an earthen wall along a hiking trail in Montenegro. Whereas his companions appeared lighthearted and smiling, Willi's brow remained furrowed, his eyes lowered, hands on his lap. He appeared deep in thought.

As the wandering youth of the *Grauer Orden* sat around a raging campfire, it is likely they shared anxious questions in their quest for personal conscience. Willi's sister Anneliese remembered that he longed for freedom to explore and to form friendships based on meaningful conversation and common values. More and more he turned away from home, focusing his attention to his youthful companions and strengthening his personal attitudes. He explained to his sister that his escape into the world did not mean that his devotion to his family lessened, but that he carried the love he had received from home with him.

Willi's troubles with the Gestapo began in the cold winter days of 1938. Shortly after his birthday on the second of January, the Nazis rounded him up along with seventeen of his *Grauer Orden* comrades, holding them in detention and subjecting them to hours of interrogation. The Special Court at Mannheim handed him an indictment of *Bündische Umtriebe*, an accusation of subversive activities within the youth movement. After three weeks of confinement during National Socialism's 1937–38 sweep to clear their house of illegal youth groups, Willi's imprisonment ended. Later he was among those granted amnesty in celebration of the annexation of Austria.

The euphoria of the *Anschluss*, the annexation of Austria, pervaded the world of National Socialism throughout Germany and Austria. German troops had marched into Austria in March of 1938, paving the way for Hitler in his black Mercedes-Benz as it headed towards his birthplace in Linz. Crowds waved bouquets of flowers, and citizens knelt to gather handfuls of dirt from the hallowed tread marks of the Führer's automobile. Many Austrians sympathized with National Socialism, believing it would introduce the prosperity it imagined Hitler had brought to Germany. As the nation celebrated, and Willi escaped further prosecution by the government, he felt more than ever the clash between his Christian faith and the goals of the Third Reich. His battles with his conscience and the regime followed him into the National Labor Service and then into the Wehrmacht.

Drafted in 1939, he trained as a paramedic. The tide of invasion pulled him into Poland and Yugoslavia in Hitler's eastern expansion for *lebensraum*, more living space for a master race. Willi's nature rebelled against the brutalities of Nazi aggression. He wore the uniform of a student-soldier, but his heart was with God and the healing art he hoped to practice as a physician. In a 1941 letter written from Russia and sent to a friend, he admitted that the sounds of shooting in the early morning were a constant reminder of the realities of another day at war.

Questions of loyalty to God and to country churned within him. More choices still lay ahead.

# Chapter Four

# ALLEGIANCES

"I SWEAR BY GOD THIS HOLY OATH. To the leader of the German Reich, Adolf Hitler, total loyalty and obedience." The oath sickened Alexander Schmorell. To solemnly and formally call upon God to witness the Nazis' truth, not the truth as he understood it, seemed an impossible demand. His induction into the army required him to submit his free will to the Führer, but he would issue a challenge. Alex approached a superior officer and dared to request a waiver of the oath requirement, stating his conscientious objection. Not surprisingly, the officer rejected his appeal. Alex conceded. He recited the words, knowing that at least he had registered his protest. Though he wore the uniform of the Wehrmacht, he had not entirely betrayed his convictions.

Compromise shadowed Alex throughout his life, sometimes enriching it and sometimes endangering it. Even the place of his birth lay somewhere between one place and another. Alex was born on September 16, 1917, in the Ural Mountains of Russia, the zone separating Europe from Asia where cultures of the East and West mingled. This fact modified his identity as a German.

Disease struck Alex's early childhood when a typhus epidemic took his mother's life. Then the toddler crawled through his first years in the specter of the Russian Revolution, and at four years old he climbed aboard a train headed for Germany with his father, Dr. Hugo Schmorell. But Russia was not forgotten. Alex's Russian nursemaid taught him the language, an echo of the culture left behind. He then became a German national with a Russian nickname, "Schurik," inheriting a worldview larger than the narrow boundaries of the Third Reich.

In his teenage years, when faced with pressures to join the Hitler Youth, Alex did not exhibit the early zeal of a boy like Hans Scholl. Neither did he have the protection of Willi Graf's alternative Catholic youth group since he had been baptized in the Russian Orthodox Church of which his maternal grandfather had been a cleric. Rather, Alex had reluctantly joined the Hitler Youth.

In 1935, good fortune crossed Alex's path when another teenager, Christoph Probst, enrolled in his school in Munich. The boy with the narrow face and light blue eyes impressed Alex with his alert, friendly, and playful manner. Quickly the two youths discovered a shared love of intellectual inquiry, a certain independence of mind, and a penchant for humor. Christoph, sometimes known as Christl, had also been a half-hearted member of the Hitler Youth, sometimes able to avoid active membership because of his frequent moves from boarding school to boarding school. At other times, he participated in the Hitler Youth activities in order to avoid being a loner in a new school.

Like Alex, Christoph's experiences reached beyond the borders of the Fatherland to places far to the east. Submersed in academia, his father, Hermann Probst, an independent scholar of Asian culture and Eastern religions, distanced himself from politics. Even so, the Probst household did not give enthusiastic support to Hitler.

Sometimes, father and son might sit together engaged in a debate, probing each other's intellect, working as a team as if playing a sport. Such dialogue provided Christoph a rich environment in which a critical attitude flourished. Although his parents had divorced when he was very young, Christoph prospered in the intellectual climate of his father's home. But that came to an abrupt end when the teenager's father, suffering from a deep depression, committed suicide.

Christoph retreated into private meditations on the meaning of death, yet, through his own grief he reached out to console his stepmother. He believed he had only lost Hermann Probst's physical presence, and the family would be reunited in the afterlife. Like his friend Alex, Christoph met with the premature death of a parent. The companionship of school friends like Alex sustained him during adolescence.

Walking along with a classmate and one of his teachers, Christoph fell into a philosophical discussion characterized by a melancholy which his friends attributed to his father's recent death. He missed his father's mentorship, but his teachers, especially a favorite, accepted him as an equal partner in intellectual conversation. The adults at the Schondorf School appreciated the scope of the teenager's knowledge from the very first day he arrived. Talent and circumstance matured him beyond his years.

Camaraderie blossomed as the boys hiked the hill country and skied along the trails of the Bavarian Alps. Christoph believed in their unbreakable friendship which deepened as he and Alex entered early adulthood. Whether attending concerts, sharing wine with friends, clowning in the dorm, or engaging in philosophical debate, the Reich caught the young men in a web of obligation.

Like Alex, Christoph submitted to the National Labor Service requirement imposed on him after his high school days. Then, he chafed at the restrictions and imperatives of military service. He balked at having to wear the Luftwaffe uniform with the eagle pinned over its right pocket and a tie knotted under the shirt's stiff collar. He became sullen and depressed, and his usual outgoing manner disappeared. Christoph did not hold a strong military attitude; it seemed contrary to an inner life rooted in his personal quest. Not strongly defined by a particular religious tradition, the young man developed a deep spirituality often reflected in letters to his siblings when he assured them that love was the power that nurtured human life and made it sacred.

Even though Alex and Christoph recited the ritual allegiance to Hitler, each found ways to console himself for yielding to conformity. When the army drafted Christoph's younger half-brother, he seemed to have reconciled the inevitability of labor service and the military to the extent that he could now offer some advice. Decades later, his brother Dieter recalled Christoph's compassion, his insight, and his early maturity. In a letter to his brother, Christoph said that the young men must endure what was imposed on them by the regime. He believed that an inner life could be preserved that remained unaffected by the events on the outside. The struggle between conscience and feelings of duty and loyalty shadowed Probst. For the time being he chose interior migration.

ALEX SCHMORELL, CHRISTOPH PROBST, WILLI GRAF, and Hans Scholl were only four of hundreds of thousands in a German military that was clearly forbidden by the terms of the Treaty of Versailles. Defiantly, Hitler had reintroduced conscription on March 16, 1935, building an army of close to 500,000.

In spring 1938, ready to reclaim lands lost to Germany after WWI, Hitler held more control over the army than any German leader since Frederick the Great. It had a different impact on Alex than it had on Willi Graf. Alex stood among those soldiers mobilized to follow the leader in one of the Reich's first targets of aggression, Austria.

Six million ethnic Germans lived in Austria, the land of Hitler's birth. The Führer pushed forward an *Anschluss,* an expansion of German territory, even though the Treaty of St. Germain prohibited the reunification of the people so that Germany's strength would not pose a threat after the Great War. Determined to restore Germany as a powerful nation, Hitler disregarded the authority of past treaties. Alex and other former Hitler youths, now soldiers in the Wehrmacht, would carry out his defiant maneuvers. Alex's endurance would be tested.

Streetcars, draped with banners bearing swastikas, clanked through German and Austrian city streets. Anticipation mounted, and *Anschluss* banners read: "Those of the same blood belong to the same Reich." Hitler dismissed the Treaty of Versailles' prohibition of rearmament and stockpiling of war machines. For the first time in twenty years a German military prepared for an offensive. The Führer deceived the world by claiming he built tractors when, for years, men worked covertly developing an armored tank called the *Panzer.*

In March 1938, Hitler tested the mobility of his forces as the army gathered, confident with its newborn capabilities. The infantry marched alongside mechanical wonders, and horse-drawn vehicles lined up behind them. The bad weather did not dampen the jubilation. Ambulances, and medics like Alex, pushed forward across the border, encountering little resistance from the Austrian population. Many of its citizens already belonged to the National Socialist Party.

Austrian crowds cheered as thousands spilled into Vienna's Heldenplatz on March 15, 1938. Standing erect at the podium rising above the throng, Hitler extended his arms forward and grasped the lectern. The Nazi swastika banner, stretched and framed, hung on a flagpole above the dignitaries standing at attention behind the Führer. The plaza, bounded by its imposing buildings, exploded with *"Heil Hitler."* In Austria, Alex witnessed the acceleration and expansion of Hitler's "Thousand Year Reich." Hitler dreamed of transforming Linz, his birthplace, into a "World City" where he and his mistress would one day retire.

The six hundred Jews of Linz fled or later vanished in concentration camps. Only twenty-seven survived.

After Austria, Hitler prepared to march the Wehrmacht into Czechoslovakia, the home of three million ethnic Germans whom he would gather into the Third Reich's fold. The Wehrmacht ignited the theory of rapid advance, speed, and concentration of force. The Führer's empire-building thrust Willi Graf forward to the frontlines and propelled Alex Schmorell and Hans Scholl toward battlefields' edges.

IN THE SPRING OF 1940, HANS maneuvered along the lines of the advancing Wehrmacht as National Socialism's massive war machine stormed towards France. Hans, a dispatch rider in a mechanized cavalry, transported messages as the Führer's army thundered out of Germany. May's warm air rushed against his body as he sped along Luxembourg's smooth roadways and through its beautiful countryside. Houses tucked in quaint, neat villages skimmed past him like the scenery on a movie screen. The benign roads transformed into obstacle courses as German convoys forged their way into Belgium. Transports churned through the landscape leaving a trail of debris behind.

Hans gripped the motorbike's throttle as he averted ditches and rock piles threatening to bring him down. His wrists swelled. The bounce of the cycle jolted his kidneys, and he shifted his weight, readjusting his attention to the hazards. Hans drove through villages where frightened refugees milled about in confusion—sad-eyed women, fearful children, and withered grandparents.

As Hans raced farther and farther away from his homeland, the bike's odometer registered the many miles. Witness to unbridled looting as the Wehrmacht crashed through European borderlands, he ached for rest.

Medical units occupied French hospitals or sometimes encamped in field hospitals close to the front or sheltered in the rear echelons. The Germans surveyed towns for billet, commandeering the best houses available. Commanders shouted evacuation orders. Terrified occupants fled as the invading army transformed French homes into barracks.

Hans' conscience protested. He wrote his parents that he would rather have a straw bed.

By early June, Hans' unit had pulled back from St. Quentin to a pastoral village remote from the battlefields. This rear echelon of the Wehrmacht's strategic lines lay at rest. Distance muffled the sounds of explosions that left a trail of hundreds of thousands wounded and tens of thousands dead. Villagers abandoned their mowing. Fields lay still. Hay grew tall and wild in the silence. Horses, untethered, roamed riderless. These hushed fields could mute treachery and offer retreat into illusions of normalcy.

A recent motorcycle crash had injured Hans' rib, and recovery time brought him into the countryside's pastures. Lying quietly in the soft, high grasses, he read or translated a book. The glorious weather during his respite energized Hans. Once, he eyed a horse moving freely under a wide sky. He could not resist approaching quietly. Then waiting for the right moment, he paced himself, and with the swift, skillful instincts of a trained equestrian, he mounted the horse. The animal spirited Hans across the vacant fields.

Near the front lines, occupying German infantry gained ground in French towns where houses with shuttered windows lined narrow cobble-stoned streets, and rigid corpses littered the roadways. Smoke rose from bombarded buildings along rivers, and German pontoon rafts ferried engineers and equipment across the waterways. Men huddled around field guns and inside cruiser tanks as the Luftwaffe swamped the Allies. In the French Alps, Italian men hung on ragged cliffs, some hugging crevices and teetering at the edges of steep inclines, all the while aiming weapons into valleys beneath the towering mountains.

In July, Hans' unit occupied a hospital near Paris where doctors, nurses, and student medics worked tirelessly; the blitzkrieg left few in its path unscathed. The experience in the field taught lessons the medical student could not have mastered from his university textbooks.

Hans wearily turned toward the door of the surgical suite. The patients' battles on the operating table were often as fierce as those on some distant field. Weakening hearts engaged in combat with horrific wounds. Hans assisted the surgeons as they sawed and chopped at bone, amputating legs severed at mid-thigh. Just one operation of this type could be an exhausting ordeal. Sometimes he attended surgical procedures twenty times a day. Daily, carts delivered soldiers with broken and crushed limbs. The young German medics, with the help of local French nurses, moved quickly, stemming hemorrhages, packing wounds, sedating pain-wracked soldiers. Frequently their efforts were in vain and life slipped away.

Sliding out the door, Hans pursed a crude cigarette between his dry lips. The tissue-thin roll lit, and red sparks flared as he deeply inhaled. Exhaling, he left a cloud of smoke swirling around his tired brain. It seemed to him an absurd response, this cigarette, while men were dying inside. When he wrote to his parents, commenting that being a healer and a soldier was an irony that did not pass unnoticed, sadness laced his message.

# Chapter Five

# SOLITUDE

SOPHIE READ BANNED BOOKS, the writings of intellectuals, philosophers, and poets. Fritz, a professional soldier and a lieutenant in the army, trained warriors for the Führer. It seemed an unlikely friendship. He became a target for her pointed questions urging him to consider the contradiction of fighting a war for which, she reminded him, he felt ambivalence. Despite frequent debates, their relationship deepened with each leave of absence and each correspondence, softening the hard edges of those difficult separations.

Sophie neatly folded the letter she dated May 16, 1940. One week ago she had turned nineteen, and Fritz had been with her in Ulm. When the Wehrmacht ordered his unit to the Low Countries, Sophie fretted: Where exactly is he? Will he be able to contact me? Is it all a secret? There were just too many farewells.

When Sophie had finished her final semester of secondary school two years earlier, Fritz transferred to Austria in 1938. Then camping trips with friends, star-gazing, and sea voyages punctuated her school days. But it was a time, too, when old Jewish neighbors and long-time classmates suddenly "emigrated." Doctors, who had taken care of Ulm's children for years, disappeared. *Kristallnacht* devastated the Jewish community as it had in countless villages and towns, yet Sophie's response is not clear. Even when Britain and France declared war on Germany in 1939, it still might have seemed somewhat remote from her life in Ulm. She tried to maintain a degree of normalcy and to divert anxious thoughts. Trips to the North Sea to jump in the rough waves energized her. Playing the piano, sketching, drawing, and her studies kept her busy, filling the void left by Fritz's departures. Often she and friends illustrated stories, both originals and classics, like that of the freedom-loving Peter Pan and the lost boys. Sophie had not yet packed away for good her BDM uniform and membership, and still she remained protected and comforted by the luxury of the Scholls' large apartment on Cathedral Square, available after another family's emigration. The streets of Ulm, filled with soldiers, demonstrations, and parades, reminded her that the war's dangers were ever present, and she worried about the men she loved, her brothers and, of course, Fritz.

For all the anxiety, there were the furloughs. By March 1940, Sophie and Fritz had shared a vacation skiing in the Allgäu hill and mountain region of Bavarian Swabia, making a long excursion via the Gemstal and the Hocap Pass in places that turned white to pink with the setting sun. Sophie wrote to her sister Elizabeth, barely able to convey the exhilaration of charging down the mountainside of soft snow packed to ice by the end of the day's runs. But furloughs ended and with it the warmth of Fritz's nearness. A month later, when images of the mountain retreat rested fresh in her memory, Sophie sent a care package to Fritz with a note imagining sharing a cup of tea in a quiet moment, comfortable and close to each other.

The letter dated May 16, now ready to be sealed and sent abroad, could not hide Sophie's gnawing wish that Fritz would not succumb to the ways of war. She would not let him be; her words stirred him. Having confessed that, she once again turned to nature to steady her—nature whose patterns remained constant amidst the increasing turmoil around her. Turning and returning to the natural world was a habit formed early in her life when she lived in the countryside in Forchten-berg. Later, when the Scholls moved to Ulm, the Danube coun-tryside was never too remote from the city limits.

The Scholl family photo collection recorded intimate moments of Sophie's delight in the earth in earlier, more inno-cent times: Sophie, head crowned with a daisy chain; Sophie sit-ting on a fence, legs dangling, eyes peering through budding branches. In another portrait Sophie had climbed a tall thin tree, wrapped her stockinged legs around its slender trunk and clung to the rough touch of its bark, sensing the life vibrating from root to canopy.

The energies of the woodland adventures lured her into tiny hidden spaces nourishing an introspection not only inspired by the forest's grandness but also by the smallest intri-cacies of the creatures living there. More snapshots captured Sophie leaning against a giant white birch or lifting a skirt to slip her feet into a pool at the base of a hillside. She drew pic-tures with words to paint what the photographs suggested, writing her love of this country and gratitude for the place called home.

Sophie struggled for balance, her musings interrupted by war's report, and thoughts deeply troubled by the betrayals of the state and individual human beings. She tried to swim and lounge, but even nature's beauty could not banish the growing terrors.

When Sophie posted her May letter to Fritz, she had already enrolled at the Fröbel Institute in Ulm. She would have preferred to be registering at the university in Munich to study biology and philosophy where Hans studied medicine as a stu-dent-soldier. That would have to wait; the Third Reich har-bored other plans for ambitious, intelligent young people like Sophie. The regime would press her into six months of com-pulsory work for the National Labor Service before permitting her enrollment in a university academic program. Sophie tried to wriggle out of the commitment by applying for kindergarten teacher training. She hoped this program would exempt her from any further service.

Sophie stretched out on her bed, glad to be home after a

hectic day of practice teaching at a local kindergarten in Ulm. She studied the two roses set in water on the table beside her bed; her thoughts wrapped around the news of France's impending surrender. She pictured the faces of the little ones in her class, wondering about their futures and hers. The patience demanded in a child's world exhausted her, though she loved her relationship with them, trying to know each well enough to meet his or her particular needs. After writing to Fritz, she drifted off to sleep.

Shortly after completing the requirement at Fröbel, a day nursery in Ulm hired Sophie. But on a late March day in 1941, she received unwelcome news—she could not escape the six months of compulsory work service in the *Arbeitsdienst*. The Reich no longer granted deferments for alternate service like kindergarten teaching.

Once again, Sophie rushed to Fritz, confiding her frustration and disappointment while at the same time calling upon her inner strength to boost her spirits. Slowly, her thoughts turned from annoyance to considerations of how she would adjust to the lack of privacy and the uniformity demanded by the regime. As she matured, she saw more clearly the twisted intentions of Hitler's promises.

A few weeks later, in early April, Sophie arrived at the Krauchenwies camp. Of all the possessions she packed for her six-month stay, a flashlight, batteries, and books would prove great comforts stored in her dormitory locker. Her diary and letters record the difficulties she encountered there. During the nights of her first week, Sophie tossed and turned in an upper bunk, trying to fight off the insomnia that plagued her. In the unseasonable cold weather she wished for the warmth of a heating pad to lull her into slumber. During her sleepless hours, mice scurried about her sleeping roommates. In those chill moments, she consoled herself with the thought that it was April and the worst of winter had disappeared.

Routines of the camp established themselves as the girls received their assignments. After work, they gathered in the dormitory laughing, cracking jokes, chatting, and complaining about the sarcastic, unfriendly supervisor. Sophie withdrew from the group. Whether precipitated by pride, conceit, or depression, she kept her distance. The trivial conversations of the other *Arbeitsdienst* girls bored her. They jabbered about the latest romance novels while she slipped Saint Augustine's *Confessions* out of her locker. She turned the pages, reading silently, deeply, and alone amid the tumult spinning around her in the old manor house, the living quarters of the girls at Krauchenwies.

In early May, flowers decorated the birthday table; twelve girls posed for the camera at Sophie's twentieth celebration. Two swigged from glass bottles and several others sipped from their ceramic cups. Only Sophie, serious and staring away from the photographer, looked like a prisoner in the striped pajamas they all wore.

For the women of the Third Reich, Hitler had but one goal—motherhood. The Nazi slogan, *"Kinder, Kirkche, Kyche"* (children, church, and kitchen) summarized women's purpose. Fewer and fewer women attended the universities; Sophie's plan to study biology and philosophy was not the norm. Education geared itself toward physical fitness and priming women for their biological roles. The Führer would prefer that she select a racially appropriate partner with whom to breed future Aryan heroes. Even when Sophie received a degree, her chances of securing a place in the professional world were slim, particularly after she married. However, if she produced four or more children, she would receive a medal and other honors befitting a heroine.

Sophie's distance from the other girls at Krauchenwies did not go unnoticed. Targeted with snide comments, Sophie knew they thought her aloof, but those perceptions did not diminish her desire to keep thoughts free and sharp. She wrote to her friend Lisa telling her she kept her reading to herself. She felt like a misfit and was very unhappy. Sophie would not allow herself to be drawn into their circle. She resisted.

Letters to and from family and friends became Sophie's lifeline, especially the self-published newsletter called the *Windlicht* (Hurricane Lamp) circulated among a small group of youths. In one edition, Sophie's friend, Otl Aicher, also the best friend of her brother Werner, had printed an essay about the philosophers Socrates, Plato, Aristotle, and spirituality. She prepared a response to his piece for publication. Through the modest journal, the young friends communicated about philosophical and spiritual issues, a sharp contrast to Nazi propaganda. In the *Windlicht,* thoughts remained free.

Time off from work meant time for outdoors in the parklands surrounding the camp's manor house. In the first days at Krauchenwies snow covered the grounds, and Sophie watched the falling flakes, waiting for a thaw so she could explore. In these woodlands she cultivated a sacred space for private meditation where her spirit could take flight or battle with deep and complex questions. Watching the deer, and later in the summer picking wild strawberries, lifted her spirits.

One late spring evening, Sophie observed clouds floating in the disappearing light as the sky turned orange from the setting sun. She refused to turn her face away from the dramatic light show, so she walked home backwards steadying her gaze on the evening's spectacle. Later that night, before going to sleep, she hid beneath the covers of her bed and secretly wrote to Fritz remembering their vacation at the North Sea when they played on the sandy beach. It was a moment gratefully retrieved.

Sophie welcomed assignment to labor in the fields away from the detested camp. She pedaled over hills and across woodlands in the Danube valley until she reached the farm where she would work for eight hours each day. Gladly, she squished through the stables. Armed with a hoe, some hours passed cultivating the earth between rows of turnips, or bending over rows of poppy seedlings, pulling weeds one-by-one from long furrows. Weary at the end of the workday, Sophie cycled through the June sunshine toward camp.

Inside the small locker where she kept personal items, Sophie pinned pictures of the cathedral spire at Ulm and some photos of her sisters and brothers. Here also she stored the books she was allowed to keep. She hadn't quite figured out the reason the dorm supervisor had taken a friendly attitude towards her and not insisted she get rid of the books the regime prohibited, titles like Thomas Mann's *Zauberberg*, works of Saint Augustine, Francis Jammes' *Ma Fille Bernadette* and others.

Augustine was a difficult companion for a girl alone in a National Labor Service camp, so there were times when she skimmed the surface of his words, while on other occasions she grasped an insight. Those moments gave her the intellectual courage to continue the philosophical inquiries that sometimes dragged her into the mire or sometimes elevated her thoughts.

Sophie longed for quick release from the camp; she felt certain she would reach old age before she ever got to the university. For weeks and months she depended upon letters from her brother Hans, sisters, and friends to keep dialogue alive. Instead of the class notebook of a college student, Sophie filled her diary with reflections on questions posed in her correspondence. The works of Saint Augustine offered some answers. Like Sophie, Augustine had been a pilgrim on a quest for God and soul, a seeker into questions of the spirit: authority, free will, belief, knowledge, and illumination. Sophie sifted through her own thoughts on questions of faith, morals, and the place of the individual within a society. Just as the medieval man had leaped into the struggle for personal faith, so had Sophie.

Drained from the labors of loading hay, some days Sophie felt rebellious. She promised herself she would smoke a protest cigarette and feel liberated in her deliberate disobedience to camp rules.

As her six months in the National Labor Service edged towards completion, Sophie counted the weeks remaining. Then came the terrible news of the Reich's sudden decision to squeeze six more months of community work from her. She dashed off a letter to Hans lamenting this latest interference. She begged her family to help her think of an escape from this fate that would ruin her dreams of study in Munich. There must be a way out. Perhaps if she studied medicine it would convince the government to release her from the assignment. She tried to hold on to hope, but by the end of August her plans melted into resignation. In November she began her work for the National Socialist Public Welfare at a Blumberg kinder-garten near the Swiss border.

Those were difficult days for Sophie. The inevitable uncertainties of her future pushed her deeper into her interior life as her journal became a space for prayer and meditation, trying to surrender to God's will. But even then, Sophie felt her spirit shriveling.

# Chapter Six

# ALLIANCES

A MOVE TOWARD FRIENDSHIP could be a move toward danger. Even though Alex Schmorell and Hans Scholl each became increasingly discontented with the regime's injustices and restrictions, how were they to know it was safe to express these views to each other? They could share talk about France; they had that in common. But Hans no longer raced motorcycles along an invasion's rutted roads, and Alex no longer drove ambulances through occupied territories. Now, in the autumn of 1940, more like students than soldiers, they turned attention to university coursework and study for medical exams.

Each young man had his reasons for devoting himself to the rigors of medicine. Alex grew up within the milieu of his father's prestigious medical practice in Munich. In deference to his father's wishes, he now pursued the same career even though his real passion was sculpture; he loved fashioning imaginative forms, working his spirit into the clay.

Hans, intrigued by the sciences, chose medical studies, but as the war progressed his interest in politics strengthened, and he entertained thoughts of someday writing what he considered the history of Germany under Nazi rule. When his father had been mayor of Forschtenberg, Hans observed Herr Scholl's skill for organizing public works projects. He believed in the betterment of community through the creative contributions of individual citizens, a vision quite unlike Hitler's concept of the Volk which destroyed individual innovation and demanded obedience to the extremes of a homogeneous community.

The Third Reich supported the studies of the student-soldiers like Hans, Alex, and Christoph, offering them stipends and often adjusting tours of duty to coincide with their semester schedules. For what were these future doctors being trained? The Third Reich had prepared SS doctors to shape and mold the human anatomy to suit its concept of the perfect society. To the Nazis, scientific research could mean performing torturous experiments in darkened rooms and secret laboratories. Dr. Mengele, barely a decade older than Alex and Hans, would collect human beings and use them as specimens to explore genetic mysteries that might lead to Hitler's dream of the perfect blue-eyed blonde Aryan. Not all of the Jewish children subjected to his experiments would survive the hand of the doctor known as the "Angel of Death."

A future in National Socialist medicine could be filled with unexpected directives.

Trust was a rarity. True intention often lay hidden beneath benign appearances: co-workers made betrayals to the Gestapo; children, brainwashed by the state's propaganda, delivered their nonconformist parents to the authorities; classmates breached their faith in each other as well as their teachers in the name of patriotism. Relationships crumbled as the Gestapo rounded up individuals whose words or actions the regime regarded as treason with the consequence of imprisonment or even death.

Informers were everywhere and a citizen lived life looking over a shoulder.

There was some safety in formal introductions, but Alex did not always exercise restraint with his sarcastic or witty remarks, and Hans' charisma and intelligence drew people to him easily. Since Jürgen Wittenstein, a fellow medical student, had brought them together, they discovered they both liked to fence and both enjoyed classical concerts at Munich's music halls. In time, they shared more conversations at places like the local Italian wine cafe. A word, a subtle action, shared daily routines and coursework, trust emerged through which Alex and Hans understood it safe to speak more openly. Alex already enjoyed the comfort and security of a long-time friend like Christoph. For minds like Hans, it was a relief when one could detect a common attitude in another; it made friendship a possibility. But that took time and could not be rushed. There were still lonely moments.

Back from the battlefield, both students had been assigned to the medical unit of the Second Student Company headquartered in Munich. The young soldiers in the barracks, even though they wore the Wehrmacht uniform, and even though drills and military routines crammed their schedules, found time for talk that mattered. Alex, a Russian Orthodox, and Hans, a Protestant, read common books such as Paul Claudel's, *The Satin Slipper*, the work of a Roman Catholic mystic and dramatist whose writings frequently examined spiritual conflict. It was this intellectual curiosity, this free-thinking spirit that drew the like-minded together.

Alex had experienced such a happy accident in Hamburg a few years earlier in 1939. Pedaling to a familiar lakeside, he found a spot to relax. Twenty-one-year-old Traute Lafrenz cycled, too, that day towards a chance meeting that neither could have known would help to shape their futures. Alex and Traute crossed paths, stopped, and then started a long conversation about a subject they both loved, literature, and in particular the Russian authors. Years later, Traute would recall that moment and reflect upon the magnetism of Alex's smile. Each may have thought that was the end of a chance encounter.

But Munich held another surprise when Traute, now a twenty-two-year-old medical student at the university and a patron of the arts, turned her head at a concert in the Odean and there he was, Alex, the sun. So it was that she became a member of a small circle growing around "reading evenings" first staged as literary salons. But the discussions: Plato,

Goethe, Lao-Tzu, Thomas Mann, and more, soon raised questions that turned talk political and turned Hans Scholl's romantic intentions toward this bright and beautiful young woman.

For Traute, such shared reflection was quite natural. During her high school years in Hamburg, her teacher, Erna Stahl, made a point of getting students to think. "She instilled in us a freer way of looking at things," Traute later recalled. At a time when young people witnessed book burnings and exposure to the brutal journalism of the Nazi news weeklies, this teacher provided a counterforce to National Socialist propaganda. Erna discouraged pupils from aligning themselves with the Hitler Youth and evaded the race question in her classes.

In 1935 at the Lichtworkschule, Stahl introduced the "reading circle." At such evening gatherings, interested pupils met to share ideas, often discussions of forbidden literature like Rilke or Shakespeare. Erna did not silence the circle when questions and criticisms about the expanding restrictions on personal and civil liberties or the discrimination of the Jews, crept into the dialogue. Not surprisingly, Erna Stahl suffered transfers, dismissals, and imprisonment for her resistant attitudes and practices. Decades later, Gerhard Casper, one of her former students and later the president of Stanford University, praised her as an educator who considered learning as "the search for truth, positive values, excellence across history and civilizations."

Having the influence of Stahl's attitudes and a history of participation in her reading circles meant Traute Lafrenz had much to offer her Munich friends. But that would weave itself into long walks, ski trips, and the shared intimacies of blossoming friendships with and without Hans Scholl.

NOT ALL TIME WAS SPENT IN THE ARMY BARRACKS since the Wehrmacht permitted student-soldiers a second residence elsewhere as long as they followed military regimens and fulfilled their service obligations. In the course of a year or two in Munich, Hans lived in a variety of student quarters, moving around like the typical college student from place to place as circumstance and convenience changed with rotations in his schedule or clerkships.

Alex's family villa, located in Harlaching, a neighborhood on the outskirts of the center of Munich, provided him with the luxuries, comforts, and privileges of home when he was not in the barracks. When Alex first brought home a study partner by the name of Hans Scholl, Dr. Hugo Schmorell considered the young man an unknown entity to approach with guardedness. After all, the tone and content of conversation in the Schmorell household might incriminate them according to Reich standards. Bringing new friends into his home was not a casual affair, especially if Dr. Schmorell's plans included a reading evening.

Regularly visitors, some contemporaries of the distinguished doctor, approached the villa for scheduled meetings. Three young men, Alex, Hans, and Christoph, joined the scholars, artists, and prestigious group of intellectuals gathered together one particular evening. Christoph, well known in the household since his high school days, was extended an open welcome, but Hans Scholl, a newcomer to these "reading evenings," had gained entry only after having established trust and familiarity with the Schmorell family. Discussions frequently centered on theology, philosophy, and literature. Often participants read their works banned or unpublished because of the restrictive policies of the government. The opportunity served as an antidote to the growing anti-intellectual environment of the Reich.

During such an evening at the villa, Alex stepped forward to introduce his two guests. Christoph and Hans greeted each other and after just a few hours, a spark of recognition ignited by common attitudes, intelligence, wit, and questions, marked the beginning of another new friendship. The villa gatherings offered a forum for open inquiry not easily available elsewhere. Alex, Christoph, and Hans would meet many times after this. Empowered by the brilliance and creativity evident at the Schmorell gatherings, the young men inaugurated their own salons, inviting select individuals to an artist's studio in Schwabing. Traute was among them.

Not all protests against the Reich remained covert as did the evening meetings of intellectuals and artists. During the summer of 1941, Clement Augustus Galen, the Roman Catholic Bishop of Munich, preached a series of sermons censuring the regime for injustices imposed on citizens in the name of a unified Germany. The bishop condemned the confiscation of monasteries and convents as these religious residences transformed into office space for government officials or sometimes homes for unwed mothers.

The bishop risked imprisonment when, from the pulpit, he denounced the Nazi euthanasia policy. Many folks, sitting in the church pews, understood Hitler's picture of the healthy Aryan; in school their children had learned Hitler's theory of race along with geography, reading, and math lessons. Nazi propaganda attempted to indoctrinate Germans with the belief that the only humane solution for the problems of the "feeble-minded," who needed constant care, was to get rid of them.

On Sunday, August 3, 1941, Bishop Galen defended the lives of the human beings whom the regime labeled, "unproductive national comrades." He condemned the regime's argument that the mentally handicapped were of no value since they did not contribute to society, reminding his listeners and readers that these individuals were part of the human family.

Parents with a mentally handicapped child housed in an asylum near Munich could lose their son or daughter in this manner: One day a van arrives at the home and their child is transported to some unknown destination. Then on a Munich spring morning, the family opens a letter informing them of the child's death from an unexpected illness.

Bishop Galen rebuked feigned excuses like this and continued his assault as the congregation before him riveted its attention to his words. The bishop commanded his flock to recognize the Reich's murderous policy as an atrocity contrary to the moral laws of God and Nature. His passion ignited as his sermon concluded, reiterating the commandment: Thou shalt not kill.

In September 1941, Hans agreed to run an errand for the Scholls' friend, Otl Aicher. Accompanied by Inge, the brother and sister traveled to Solln, arriving at a handsome house on Emil-Dittler-Strasse. It was the season of change, and Hans would soon be celebrating his twenty-third birthday on the 22nd of September, the first day of autumn. For the last month he had noticed the fading roses and thought of the grain fields turning golden; he was acutely aware of summer's lingering fragrance. Hans may have thought this delivery a simple interruption to his life as an intern at the hospital at Harlaching just south of Munich where he made the rounds taking blood, giving intravenous injections, performing aspirations and other routine procedures.

The old man heard someone at the door. One can imagine him moving among the disarray of a house bulging with a lifetime collection of books and journals, some yellowing with age. He, too, had changed and time was turning his hair white. In 1941 nothing remained the same in the Germany he once knew. As he drew closer to the door, he walked past piles and piles of literary works, many now shut tight by the *Redeverbot* of the Third Reich, forbidden to be read or published in public. The presence of great minds had always been his companions, and much of their spirit lined the walls and filled the spaces of his home. Plato, Goethe, Paul Claudel, a gathering of artists, poets, theologians, and philosophers shared the hearth with Professor Muth. Spiritual resistance to what he called the evils of the regime defined his unorthodox views. His home on the outskirts of Munich protected much of what National Socialism forbade.

When Professor Muth opened the door, the elderly scholar saw the face of a young man—a high forehead framed by a shock of wavy thick hair, and dark eyebrows forming a bridge spanning his eyes. It was an angular face chiseled with strength and intelligence; beside him stood a young woman.

Hans greeted the gentleman. The professor learned the reason for the youths' visit and then invited them to enter. Hans delivered the bust of Pascal as instructed by Otl. The professor placed it in his studio. There was some pleasant conversation, but only later would they learn that optimism, hope, and determination were the significant exchanges that would pass among them. Inge, who accompanied her brother that day, believed luck brought exceptional people into her brother's life.

Carl Muth was a progressive Catholic thinker and editor of the journal, the *Hochland*, recently banned by the Nazis. It valued the humanizing and spiritualizing influences of the arts and religion on human society; its premise ran counter to all the Nazi culture's brutalizing forces. Muth's home had become a base for spiritual resistance where other thinkers who opposed the National Socialist system gathered to keep the embers of the "other Germany" alive. Among the contributors to his publication was Theodor Haecker, a convert to Catholicism and a man unafraid to confront the establishment, secular or religious. As a writer, translator, and cultural critic, his works remained circumspect and finally banned by the regime. That same September when the Reich ordered Jews to wear a yellow Star of David to set them apart, Haecker mourned such persecution in the journal he faithfully kept.

When Hans left Muth's vast library that day, he was invited to return.

As the colorful fall days shortened and the air grew colder, Hans settled down in the secluded attic room he rented just outside Munich. There he distanced himself from the constant troubles of the city and reserved time for contemplation and reading. The generous allowance he received from his parents, along with government stipends, afforded him a comfortable living as he pursued his university studies. Almost daily, he ventured forth along the roads to Professor Muth's to assist the old man. He spent hours in the literary retreat cataloguing collections gathered in the voluminous library. The books and magazines sated Hans' appetite for thinking and fueled questions of morality, individual responsibility, and human values—especially the relationship of justice, power, and the state.

At the end of early winter days in 1941, Hans often returned to his solitary attic room to continue his reading. A samovar hummed as it brewed tea, taking the chill out of approaching winter storms and subduing his restlessness.

Each time he returned to the journalist's house, Hans had the opportunity for stimulating conversation. For years Muth's journal, the *Hochland*, had been the medium of communication among German Catholic intellectuals entertaining topics as art, poetry, and spiritual matters, not afraid, though, to challenge the religious status quo. The Reich regarded such literature as poison. Its preservation in Muth's secret library protested the dehumanizing influences of Nazism. Though silenced as others had been, Muth's collection did not suffer the destruction of other libraries throughout Germany and the occupied areas; his shelves remained full, not emptied. Hans had access to all of them.

For years the Reich had continued its campaign to rid the Fatherland of "un-German" thought. As early as May 1933, students had marched with torchlights through the streets of Berlin. At midnight trucks hauled hundreds of volumes into the Opera-Platz where thousands of onlookers lined the way screaming, "*Heil*," and demonstrators hurled books into the heat of the bonfire. The flames burned generations of learning and culture. Scriptures curled and melted into ash while the inferno consumed the writings of Jewish authors. Bookshelves stood empty in the places where students once fed upon the pages of a nourishing literary inheritance.

Eight years after the midnight fires in Berlin, Hans faithfully reported for his duty as organizer of the old man's texts and manuscripts, knowing that it would take months to sort and classify the extensive library. By the late gray days of November, he burrowed into the project. The professor's bronchitis worsened as the coughing and wheezing weakened him. Hans suspected the stress of Third Reich policies contributed to the aging man's sickness; the anti-Jewish decrees and actions in Germany and the occupied territories burdened his mind and distressed his spirit.

ALEX, TOO, GREW UNEASY and turned to his friend Lilo with questions of conscience. They found it easy to unload their worries and to frankly share anxieties triggered by a diseased government dedicated to the destruction of basic human rights. Neither Alex nor Lilo was blind to suffering. As they sipped red wine and broke bread at a favorite wine café, the question remained: What was one to do? How does one align attitude, conscience, and response? Her husband Otto had gone off to the battlefields reluctantly, but a transformation had taken place so that she hardly recognized the voice in his letters that spoke of pride in service and the will to fulfill his soldierly duties to the utmost. The shift in his perspective stunned her.

In a letter to a girlfriend Rose, Hans confessed his own spiritual crisis. He sorted and stacked and created order in Carl's household, yet he grappled with organizing and balancing the order in his own life. The young man sank deeper and deeper into self-reflection. Letters passed back and forth between him and his mother, sisters Sophie, Inge, and Elisabeth, as well as his brother Werner and friends like Otl, his contacts with a world outside himself.

Parcels arrived and departed. Book deliveries became a veritable network of literary voices and ideas that traveled between Hans and those close in spirit. Wrapped in paper, the shipments were labeled, stamped, passed hand-to-hand, carted on trucks, and unloaded, finally arriving at their destination. The reader unwrapped and untied them, soon opening the cover and turning the pages silently. Letters etched on bound pages, formed words, and released thoughts, exercising their power over time and space, stirring the imagination, fortifying intention, fueling energy, and activating spirit. This book exchange represented a deliberate disobedience to Nazi codes and decrees.

Two books received from Werner, *Pensees* by Pascal and *Les Fleurs du mal*, satisfied Hans' enthusiasm for French literature, one he shared with Professor Muth. He offered to send his brother Etienne Gilson's writings about St. Augustine and suggested he consider the *Divine Comedy*. As a gift for his friend Otl, he chose a work of Nikolai Berdyaev who emphasized creative human life and its importance for the ongoing creation of the world. Humankind, the writer believed, could help to mend the world and collaborate with God once creative potential had been sufficiently activated. The arts would bring about a healing and unification of the heart and mind. The author's thoughts rang true to Hans who felt the arts were no luxury but rather a necessity. Hans relished the approach of yet another concert, the Bach Festival and the performance of the six Brandenburgs. A Brandenburg transformed and energized him each time he listened.

In his personal copy of one of the Russian philosopher's books, Hans inscribed the biblical admonition and warning about the efficacy of the sword. It appears that at twenty-three years old, Hans had turned from the Dagger of Honor of his Hitler Youth days and its inscription, "Blood and Honor."

A selection from Berdyaev seemed appropriate for Otl Aicher who had been deprived of a high school diploma because he refused to join the Hitler Youth. When the Reich stole his educational opportunities, Carl Muth became the boy's mentor and teacher. The young man persisted and pursued his own self-education by reading these forbidden books that later circulated like blood through the hearts of his friends.

Otl educated himself, but he also opened doors for Hans and a small group of youths by initiating the self-published newsletter called the *Windlicht*. It was a space of freedom where Hans, Otl, Sophie, Inge, Traute, and several others could write poetry, essays, and reflections as well as exhibit original artwork, empowering them to mold and shape intellect and imagination. As Inge Scholl confirmed in her accounts, they were attempting to construct a spiritual basis that would fortify them against the degrading system gripping Germany. Inge's support of the Hitler Youth movement and the prestigious status she enjoyed among the Ulm BDM women diminished. The young contributors to the *Windlicht* sometimes copied poets' works not easily accessed elsewhere because of Nazi prohibitions. The youths also had a forum to experiment with Muth's and Haecker's models, imitating the themes common to both: social justice, economic welfare, and war and peace. On a late October day in 1941, Hans wrote to Otl inviting him into a dialogue about poverty, a topic inspired by the works of Leon Bloy and Muth. Later, in November, his essay "On Poverty" was published in the *Windlicht*.

Soon Muth invited Hans to share simple meals with him.

Carl's door remained open to others who also needed free speech nourished around his dining table.

By early December 1941, Hans made a decision to leave his medical studies for the winter and direct his attention to philosophy. His focus narrowed to questions of the inner life like the season around him, the season that stored its energy in hidden underground places. Hans spent cold nights with the samovar, drawing boiling water from the spigot and brewing hot tea. He passed solitary hours reading books on loan from Muth, books with titles like Berdyaev's *Philosphie der Freiheit*. Hans drew closer and closer to the circle of minds lying beneath the icy waters of National Socialism. He, Alex, Christoph, Sophie, and Traute edged toward the threshold of the "secret Germany."

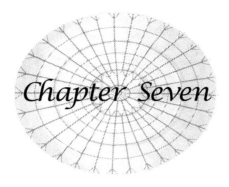

# Chapter Seven

# RESOLUTIONS

E VEN MORE EXPERIENCED MOUNTAINEERS may have delayed the
excursion, but a small band of skiers forged through the forest and up the mountain slope, nearly approaching the tree line.
Hans, Sophie, Inge, Traute, and a few other friends formed a
thin, slow-moving line, a thread of energy weaving itself
through dense fibers of blizzard snow.

Almost to the top of the treacherous climb, Hans, his coat
covered in white, turned and urged the others to the summit.
The storm failed to quell his enthusiasm even while it begged
reason to turn back. Risk had its rewards at the Coburg Cabin—
peace and security, real and imagined. Little thought was given
to the alternatives.

In the hut's center a wood-burning stove radiated comfort. A candle illuminated the pages of Dostoevsky's *The Double*
as the young men and women read together in semi-darkness.
The refuge of the next few days would inspire future articles in
their circular, *Windlicht*, where Inge Scholl praised the hide-
away as a shelter from the mad, cold world swirling around
them. Skiing the slopes by day, singing and reading around the
stove by night, the intimate circle of friends approached New
Year's Eve 1941.

Preparations for the celebration were underway as Inge and Sophie cooked a special meal for the hungry group gathered around a simple wooden table decorated with fresh evergreens. Had they not, on another evening, wrestled with questions of spiritual hunger? Like a run down the mountain, moods shifted and turned in drifts frivolous and deep. After the New Year's Eve dinner, they celebrated the hush of darkness with a reading from Novalis, an early German Romantic poet. Midnight arrived. Under a canopy of stars the young celebrants greeted the New Year 1942.

ON THE EASTERN FRONT, troops battled with the advance of a severe Russian winter. Some German soldiers, still wearing summer uniforms in weather dropping to -73 degrees Fahrenheit, froze to death at their posts when they fell asleep. A few short hours of light relieved the long, dark nights. Boiling hot soup froze in less than sixty minutes. A week before Christmas of 1941, Willi Graf had served as a medic in the Russian lands not only occupied by the Germans, but lands imprisoned by snow and stillness. In a letter to his friend Marita, he observed that one could get lost in the snow's heavy blanket.

Nothing would thwart the Führer's desire to steal Russia's power. Even though Hitler had signed a non-aggression pact with the Soviet Union, he broke the agreement, just as he had ignored the terms of the Treaty of Versailles. After numerous battlefield tours of duty—Poland, France, and Yugoslavia, the Wehrmacht had issued Willi Graf orders for Russia with Operation Barbarossa, the largest land attack ever mounted in the history of warfare.

After recovering from the persistent spring rains of 1941 that had bogged down the troops and equipment, the Germans had finally set out with their summer gear and Panzer MKIII's speeding over flat, golden plains. They captured enormous numbers of Russians, forcing them into slave labor and marching them in wide columns that snaked around Russian hamlets. German soldiers hunkered down in small towns, wrenching families from their homes and forcing them to evacuate. Men, women, and children clutched a few valued possessions; the rest they abandoned. Willi walked around an almost empty village. Little remained that hinted of life, except a cat slipping its way around piles of debris. Noticing this last speck of the past, he fed the stray survivor, maybe for the same reasons he would stop to water a few plants wilting in that wasteland.

Believing that Operation Barbarossa would destroy Russia before the seasons changed, Hitler had delayed issuing appropriate winter equipment for the Wehrmacht. Instead the Germans met with unforeseen resistance, and now troops battled with the advance of a severe Russian winter. Heat overtook concerns of war, and warmth became happiness. Willi pulled closer to a huge oven in the center of a Russian house, for a short time forgetting the cold. His thoughts turned to home, his medical studies, and longing for conversation with friends. There was no one on this December evening with whom he could read Dostoevsky; there was little room to store great books. As he finished his letter to Marita, he reminisced about his time in Bonn. Then he signed the letter as he frequently did, "Just Me."

In Germany's cities, propaganda fueled an image of the Russian as a sub-human. But the Russian beasts, as the Nazis referred to them, had the advantage of knowing the terrain and being acclimated to it. Their skilled ski units, clad in white smock camouflage, appeared swiftly for battle with weapons manufactured to resist the harsh elements that would have paralyzed them otherwise.

The weather crippled the Wehrmacht. Willi tended to men battling frostbite or struck with dysentery, waiting endless hours for supplies that needed to be shipped hundreds of miles. Vehicles refused to start and weapons froze. Some men committed suicide rather than endure any more.

Terror had torn through the Soviet Union in the year past. Savagery had overcome compassion. As another new year rushed in, memories of the war reached across the vast Russian night. Three months earlier, on the 29th of September, 1941, posters had hung around the city of Kiev ordering Jews to assemble at eight o'clock in the morning. Led along cobblestoned streets of the city, the unsuspecting crowd had marched past corpses rotting at the curbside. One man turned his head to stare at the remains; others looked straight ahead, avoiding the sight. Lines formed near a railroad as men, women, and children, singing religious songs, arrived at a ravine. Men, certain to have the money and documents required for "resettlement," waited alongside young women and children dressed in layers of warm clothing and carrying bags laden with food. Older women may have guarded jewelry and other valuable heirlooms in coat pockets or purses.

The *Einsatzgruppen* and the Ukrainian militia began the work for which they had trained and now expected generous reward. Systematically, the Special Forces, considered by the Nazis as men of valor, carried out Hitler's orders for "the separation and further treatment of...all Jews." Bread, wine, watches, rings, fur coats—the commandos robbed the Jews of their possessions and created great piles of confiscated goods. The Jews' singing turned to screams as the commandos herded mothers, fathers, daughters, sons and grandparents through a narrow pathway lined with *Einsatzgruppe C* militia and attack dogs. Walled in by a force bent on solving the Reich's "Jewish Problem," terrified families shoved forward. Those who stumbled were prey for dogs or victims of human stampede. Harsh voices ordered the now naked victims toward the edge.

Shots rang out. Two little girls and thousands of others fell into the mass grave at Babi Yar. In two days the *Einsatzgruppen* and Ukrainian militia liquidated 33,700 Jews. Later the Reich decorated the leader of the massacre, Paul Blobel, with the Iron Cross, Germany's highest award for valor. Babi Yar heralded a pattern of extermination by the *Einsatzgruppen* sweeping through occupied territories, murdering Jews, partisans, and anyone resisting the invading German Wehrmacht. Despite freezing temperatures, the massacres persisted, and the Reich's heroes procured fur coats and collected money from the pockets and purses of the dead. Nothing stopped them.

Willi beheld the opposite of love—hate and its companion, brutality. In a February 1942 letter, he confessed to his sister Anneliese that he had seen maneuvers which he wished he had never witnessed.

IN MUNICH THAT WINTER, Wehrmacht commanders held Alex and his entire unit hostage in the student company barracks for four weeks of disciplinary confinement. The young medical students groaned and complained that the restrictions interfered with their private lives. Alex despised the constraints; he balked at being in the army and avoided wearing his uniform whenever he could. Sometimes his emotions triggered an impulsive protest. In February 1942, charges of mutiny threatened him and his comrades. In a letter to the Scholls, Hans, another detainee, reported that tension mounted as those charges reached the High Command.

The medical students' trouble began during a lecture delivered by a devoted Nazi professor. After entering the room and in the course of his presentation there was a stir in the hall; some discontent sparked a commotion. A derisive outcry against the teacher came from the students assembled.

Unable to identify who among the medical students had provoked this demonstration, the commanders quarantined the entire group. Alex's reputation for speaking his mind may have singled him out as a strong suspect. The investigation remained a military affair, even though Army officers and the Gestapo sometimes vied for superior jurisdiction in matters involving soldiers. The captains guarded their men, claiming they were not subject to the directives of another authority. The Gestapo challenged the claim of the military leaders who were more likely to let some illicit conversation or a dissident remark slide past them. The unit escaped court martial and survived the quarantine. Alex and his army buddies laughed when he suggested that one day a marker on the barracks' door would memorialize the spot where organized resistance began—a resistance from within the Wehrmacht.

HANS TURNED THE KEY in the lock and opened the door of the back building at Leopoldstrasse 38. The early spring sunlight filtered through the windows, illuminating the studio belonging to Manfred Eickemeyer, an architect who during the past two years had actually been in Munich only several months.

Hans met the man when both were among guests in Carl Muth's circle. While working on construction projects in occupied Poland and Russia, Manfred witnessed the work of the *Einsatzgruppen* and returned to Germany desperate to report what he had seen, but to whom? He told Muth and others he needed to link up with someone who could do something. He needed to reveal the atrocities perpetrated against the Jews. He chose twenty-three-year-old Hans. Eickemeyer spoke, and Hans listened.

In the spring of 1942, a plain white envelope appeared in the Scholls' Ulm mailbox. When its content was unfolded, it uncovered reproduced excerpts from Bishop Galen's sermons. Even though the Reich had considered his speeches traitorous, the Gestapo did not initially pursue Bishop Galen because of Hitler's reluctance to engage in a major confrontation with the Church. When Hans learned about the handbill, he felt some satisfaction knowing that conscience had surfaced, and that someone had the courage to spread Galen's words. A duplicating machine seemed a powerful idea. Weapons manufactured to fight an armed enemy proved useless against ideological foes. Hitler hated the intellectuals, old or young; their non-conformity and individualism made them National Socialism's enemies from within. While some could be bought through greed and the promise for power, others remained immune to the pressures of Nazi propaganda. Months of work at Muth's library, readings and discussions at the Schmorells' villa, Bishop Galen's public protests, and Eickemeyer's revelations paved the way for what was to come.

HANS MOVED TOWARD THE STAIRS descending into the studio's basement. Underground and remote, the room felt secret. Both Hans and Alex responded to Eickemeyer's information with a sense of urgency, but moving forward with the plan carried grave risks. Why even Otl's adventure into the publication of the *Windlicht* had been abandoned when he and his friends learned it could lead to imprisonment of up to sixteen years for producing what the Reich would label the activity of an illegal youth group. Sixteen years for printing essays on poverty, memoirs of vacations, and copies of favorite poems, seemed too great a price to pay. The *Windlicht* enterprise disbanded. But Eickemeyer's studio opened a space for other possibilities.

Waiting to register outrage would be shameful.

The European intelligentsia sometimes detached themselves from practical participation in politics and government, finding security in the protective bubble of scholarship. No doubt Alex and his friends, Christoph and Hans, benefited from the tutelage of writers, artists, doctors, and philosophers whose company they shared at clandestine meetings. It was true that Carl Muth had registered his own protest by refusing to use Hitler's name even once in the entire thirty year history of his now banned journal, *Hochland*, but Alex and Hans felt a growing impatience with the lack of an organized opposition.

By 1942, even Christoph had shown his frustration when he confessed, "We have to do it. We have to show our attitude...that it isn't the end of freedom for the people. We have to risk this 'no' against a power that raises itself above all people and which wants to kill all resistants. We have to do it for life's sake. This responsibility can't be taken away by anyone else. National Socialism is the name of a mental illness which has infected our people."

SYMBOLS ABOUNDED IN NAZI GERMANY. Swastikas, lightning bolts, and eagles decorated the nation's flags, uniforms and public buildings. The young dissidents chose their own signature, the White Rose. Hans Scholl later explained it was selected at random. Others suggest B. Traven's novel, *La Rosa Blanca*, narrating the story of Mexican peasants defending their hacienda against a giant oil trust, inspired the name. Inge Scholl preferred to draw a parallel between the whiteness of the rose and the whiteness of a blank sheet of paper whose significance did not escape Hans. Still again, Lilo shared a letter with Alex in which a friend had written of the white rose's symbolism:

purity, death, and eternal youth. She believed the image impressed her friends.

In the spring of 1942, Alex and Hans took the first steps toward active resistance. Once again, the two young men sat across from each other, but this time it was not to study for the medical exams. Now they struggled to find the right words to call Germans to resistance. Each formulated his own version of the essential message, infusing the text with his unique voice. Then they read to each other and culled from each draft what best represented their common purposes. Intellect, spirit, and emotion poured into the collaboration of another draft, which became the first leaflet of the White Rose.

Alex's attempts to buy a copy machine ended at an obscure shop whose proprietor made a generous profit from the sale. Alex handed over the cash acquired by pooling monthly army stipends plus some extra from the personal allowance his father gave him. In Alex's room, or behind a closed door in Hans' apartment, or even in the recesses of Eickemeyer's basement, they could now test their resolve; the second-hand duplicator would not remain idle for long. Sentences began to form as they debated the language and intent of their message. To whom would they send the handbill? How would they reproduce it? How could they get enough paper and postage stamps? How would they finance the leaflets?

Hans inspected the masters that had been cut by Alex's typewriter. An artist friend, William Geyer, taught them how to work with stencils, though he did not know the nature of their project. This work demanded secrecy and discretion; knowledge, even without participation, could incriminate an individual associated with resistance. Summer had arrived and life in the student quarter, the army barracks, the hospitals, the classrooms, the concert halls, and in their families' homes carried on. But in the quiet shadows, *Widerstand*, resistance, was born.

## Concepts of Leaflet of the White Rose I

Alex and Hans shed their uniforms, rolled up their sleeves, and pressed the mimeograph's crank into their palms. With the master completed, and the machine primed, production of the first Leaflet of the White Rose began.

Where were the checks and balances to offset or derail a corrupt leadership? They continued, using the voice of the White Rose to prophesy shame for the nation, anticipating the day when the future would reveal the criminal, dark side of Germany.

The youths moved forward, taking a stand for humans' free will and chiding those who would allow their individuality to be swallowed up by a soulless mass. The leaflet described the trapped spirit energy of a nation imprisoned by the regime, a loss accomplished surreptitiously over time. It argued the people had been sleeping or hypnotized or anesthetized, no longer alert or attentive to reality. Yet, the writers recognized the awakening of a conscious few and demanded that each participate in immediate resistance to fascism.

The leaflet then reflected lessons the student-soldiers had learned from their reading of great literature and philosophy. The voice turned to Schiller and "The Lawgiving of Lycurgus and Solon," and a discussion of the ancient sages' concept of law, power, security, and the purposes of the state and the service an individual owes to that state. In Schiller's excerpt, Alex and Hans seem to have borrowed a way to say: I love my country, but what if it asks me and others to sell our souls? They used their classroom learning to suggest that history had already shown, in ancient Sparta, that to supplant love and spirit and replace them with civic virtue alone was to distort human nature. Neither the name of Hitler nor the name National Socialism appeared in the first Leaflet of the White Rose, yet their signatures were threaded throughout the text.

The closing challenge, "to resist," lent a prophetic tone by referencing a legendary Greek "seer," Epimenides, whose story suggested two levels of consciousness, that of sleep and that of wakefulness. Classic Greek traditions hold that Epimenides fell into unconsciousness as a boy, isolated in a cave that became his incubator for fifty-seven years; the time of his awakening finally arrived. Then filled

*with knowledge and wisdom, he proclaimed through poetry and*
*prophesy the themes of purification and sacrifice. Alex and Hans*
*made use of the ancient story by borrowing Goethe's words from his*
*work, "The Awakening of Epimenides," Act II, Scene 4, ending with*
*a rally call for "Freedom!"*

Though he shared their sentiments, when Christoph read what his friends had written, he objected to its elaborate language and artistic appeal, arguing it was not direct enough to reach the common person. But the authors intended to send this first message to a target audience: teachers, clergy, bookstore owners, and others who had access to the minds of the larger population.

By this time, the Reich had transformed centers of learning, and especially the university in Munich, into hotbeds of National Socialism where the state exerted control over faculty and student body. As early as 1933 the Civil Service purge of Jews applied to universities, and schools lost as many as ten per cent of their valuable members. Some of the remaining faculty, in the early years of Hitler's regime, thought of Nazism as a passing fad; others embraced it. Now, professors with a suspect attitude ran the risk of losing their livelihoods.

But there were some teachers who the young dissidents believed could be reached through their protest, perhaps someone like Kurt Huber. They had seen him step up to the lectern and felt his powerful personality. They had listened attentively, careful not to miss a reference that affirmed their belief that Hitler rattled him, too. It was not uncommon for German students to follow a professor with whom they wanted to establish a working relationship. Jürgen Wittenstein had done just that with Huber already. This professor of musicology, psychology, and philosophy often filled his lectures to capacity, some attendees present simply to audit. While Huber's speech sometimes slowed or slurred as the result of an illness, he skillfully managed to convey a subtle, critical attitude toward the regime while at the same time reflecting his love and admiration for German culture. A copy of the White Rose leaflet would go to an individual like Professor Huber.

When the old machine turned silent and still, the first production had issued approximately one hundred copies whose last lines called upon readers to: Please make and distribute as many copies of this leaflet as possible. The work had begun.

# Chapter Eight

# CONVERGENCE

IN A CITY OF NEARLY HALF A MILLION PEOPLE, Willi sometimes felt lonely. His assignment to the Second Student Company brought him to Munich, not Bonn where he had begun his medical studies. Upon his return from Russia, there were no soldiers parading through the Brandenburg Gate of Berlin, no young girls tossing bouquets as they had done two years earlier when the blitzkrieg's subjugation of France swelled streets with celebrants. Operation Barbarossa, though scoring some victories, was no lightning battle.

Willi readjusted to the rhythms of student life at the Ludwig-Maximilians-University. After the lectures of a full academic week, he would begin the next with Sunday Mass. Later in the day, he could devote time to letter writing to friends, his sisters, or to Marita. From Poland to Russia to Munich, Willi corresponded faithfully with Marita, sometimes lamenting that distance, the war, and lapses of time interfered with a continuity that might have deepened their friendship.

At the northern end of Munich's Ludwigstrasse stood the *Siegestor*, the Victory Arch, a martial monument honoring the Bavarian Army, also the entryway onto Leopoldstrasse, where the students in Schwabing gathered. Sitting alone at a sidewalk table, a student could pour over a book, edit an essay, or sweat over notes before an exam. Nearby, a table of card players might laugh and bluff their way through the kings, queens, and hearts. Thirsty for each other's company, a couple deep in conversation, may have stolen time to meet for some bread and wine. Others still, hidden behind the newsprint of the day, informed themselves of the latest reports of parades, rallies, or honors bestowed upon the Reich's Volk.

Willi broke up his studies with bike trips through the *Englischer Garten*, once a military reserve but now a sprawling public park at the edge of Schwabing. Other afternoons or evenings after lectures at the university or roll calls at the barracks, he might go to the cinema. Occasionally, he arranged time with a friend to browse through Munich bookstores, probably the old second-hand shops that might have shelved in some dusty corner a title that escaped Hitler's purge. Sometimes he contacted old friends from Saarbrücken with whom he could share Romano Guardini's ideas of liturgical reform; such discussions of changes in church ritual fostered innovative thinking.

Willi yielded to the life of the student-soldier in the Second Student Company; participation in music and sporting events separated him from the dismal battlefields of recent experience. In the spring of 1942, Willi's witness to the brute forces of combat gave way to the agility, quick thinking, and concentration of fencing, a traditional elite sport among university students in Germany. He changed his military uniform to the ritual white garb of the athlete and stood "On Guard" in preparation for an assault, the friendly combat between two fencers.

Christoph Probst loved the sport too: the presentation, the counter-attack, the conversation, the back and forth play of the blades, the precision, and the discipline. In the old days, crisscross scars on a student's face were hailed as signs of earned manhood. Fencing was a natural fit for the self-confident and fearless Christoph who met a good match when he faced Willi.

Besides participation in athletics, opportunities to frequent the concert halls and theaters pleased Willi. As spring brought new life to Munich, he could feast on Mozart, Brahms, and above all, his favorite Beethoven. Echoes of the battlefield subsided. Willi and Christoph's paths would cross again in their singing and their love of music.

Unlike Willi, though, Christoph had found a life partner, Herta. Already the marriage brought two little boys upon whom the young father lavished his affections. Music had brought the couple together on an evening several years earlier in the late 30's when the piano concert of Edwin Fischer filled the hall at the Odeon. These were Herta's warm memories of their first meeting: After the first half of the performance, the audience spilled into the hallway, and Herta spotted her brother accompanied by a handsome young man. Christoph Probst stretched out his arms to greet Herta as if he had been waiting forever to meet her. After the brief intermission, the young people returned to their places in the auditorium.

At the conclusion of the concert, Herta and her companions went to the *Hungaria*, a local eatery, only to discover Christoph already there with his mother. He invited Herta to join them for a glass of wine—the beginning of a love story.

In 1942, with a third child on the way, Christoph took caution by keeping his family away from Munich where bombers raided the city with increasing frequency. In the country he could play with his toddlers, posing for the camera to capture the happy moments: He swooped up his son and perched him on his shoulders, gripping the boy's ankles and securing him tightly for the ride. Christoph turned his head and looking upwards, caught a smile on the chubby face.

In another snapshot Herta and Christoph cuddled dark-haired Michael propped upright and cozy in his stroller. Then the camera captured more candids: Christoph snuggled one of the boys inside his knapsack and carried him on his back. Stretching out on a blanket in a field of wildflowers, he exuded contentment as his son crawled over him.

Christoph knew intimately of the need for extreme care in family matters. Not all people in Germany enjoyed the student-soldiers' freedoms and the "normal" life of the cafe table or family escapes to the foothills. Behind closed doors and shaded windows, in the shadows of life's daily routines, his stepmother remained protected in forced anonymity. She was Jewish according to the definitions formulated by the Nuremberg Race Laws of 1935. Whether or not she attended synagogue, and whether or not she was a member of a known Jewish family, she was subject to classification as a Jew. Hitler's Reich determined Jewishness as a matter of race, not a matter of religion. She could not prove her Aryan ancestry back to 1750, nor would she be able to pass the test for the Law for the Protection of German Blood and German Honor.

Christoph's sister Angelika remembered the shock of the deportations and the discovery of the brutal treatment inflicted upon the Jews. Fear haunted the family.

In order to designate a person's race, the Nazis created charts showing labels of "Full Jew", a person with three Jewish grandparents. *Mischlinge* (Germans of mixed race) of two degrees: First degree—two Jewish grandparents; second degree—one Jewish grandparent. Christoph's half-Jewish stepmother, by these determinations, would be stripped of her German citizenship and subject to disposal by the regime.

The branding of Jews with a yellow Star of David enraged Christoph. The whispers of atrocities, of concentration camps, the secrets of the Reich's euthanasia program, and the fate of the mentally ill and handicapped stalked him.

Christoph's stepmother retreated into the corners of her home. Family and friends who knew her never admitted her identity to anyone. She rarely went outdoors, and the rest of the family provided for her needs. They hoped the named "Probst," properly Aryan, would mislead the persecutors.

Being a sergeant medic in the Luftwaffe, Christoph did not share in the barracks life of the Second Student Company. Instead, he traveled to Munich from Innsbruck, often meeting with his friends Alex Schmorell and Hans Scholl and occasionally visiting at Lilo's. Sometimes they would be together for the practices of the Bach Choir. Here, too, Willi Graf lent his voice to the sacred music as a member of the vocal ensemble. Exper-

imenting with Bach's repertoire of cantatas, motets, and other
works, moved and empowered him. It also introduced him to a
circle of new friends with whom he felt he could sustain a
deeper relationship. Willi chose friends cautiously; his reticence
contributed to his reputation for being reserved and cool. He
listened to Christoph and Alex and Hans and quietly searched
their attitudes. As he began to experience a feeling of community with these new acquaintances, he eased himself closer.
Willi did not yet know of the leaflet campaign, but soon he'd
join the reading circle at Eickemeyer's studio or at Hans' place.

HANS ALSO READJUSTED TO LIFE IN MUNICH during late spring of
1942. Earlier, in March, he had served a month-long internship
in a base hospital's surgical unit in Schrobenhausen, a rural
town in Upper Bavaria, forty miles north of Munich. While
there, he sometimes spent lunch hours stretched out on the
sunny terrace, his long hair toppling over his forehead. A restless spirit shadowed him. Perturbed by the regime's expanding
surveillance, he complained in a letter to his parents about suspected mail censorship. His agitation provoked a barrage of
insults leveled at those who might pry into the soldiers' private
lives. In a sarcastic twist, he wondered how brave those same
men would be if they had to pick through wounds of battle-
torn soldiers, as he had.

   With that month behind him, Hans made his way again
to Professor Muth's house in Solln, happy to be there almost
every day. But he continued to feel uneasy, distracted, and anxious, unable to focus his affections, wondering if he would ever
be happy in love. Traute may have surmised this already, but
his attentions to other women and their fading romance did not
stop her from the Eickemeyer studio evenings. If Hans had difficulties with his love life, his heightened enthusiasm for the
leaflet project did not falter, even if Alex or Christoph might
have some reservations.

   The convergence of like minds tightened the small circle
of Munich students. They formed their own thoughts in a city
familiar with ideological battles. Munich had witnessed
Hitler's Putsch in 1923 when he came storming into town,

marching on the *Feldherrnhalle,* determined to seize power in Bavaria. Then the police overcame the instigators, and after a trial, Hitler, imprisoned for nine months, dictated his autobiography, *Mein Kampf.* Nineteen years later in 1942 the Führer pushed even harder for a programmed and homogeneous society for the next thousand years.

A return to Munich meant an occasional cup of coffee or glass of wine with friends at a café where brief exchanges fortified the young men's resolve to offer passive resistance to a tyrannical government. They camouflaged talk of gathering in the night at Eickemeyer's studio or Hans' room or Alex's house where they could read, carry on their discussion about truth, justice, and freedom, and plan the next move.

When Christoph returned to his family after a foray into Munich, he sometimes seemed like another man to Herta. It took some time for his drawn face to return to its usual mirthful expression.

Alex, too, needed an outlet for the mounting stresses accompanying his trips to the battlefield and the return to the covert work. He retreated often to Lilo's apartment. As an artist she understood how therapeutic creativity could help one transcend pain and confusion. At her place Alex might have a smoke or maybe just hold the pipe's bowl without even putting a match to the tobacco. His habitual use of the pipe, thought Lilo, represented another expression of his unwillingness to conform. She knew Alex was a seeker who sometimes acted on impulse. Steady Christoph had often anchored him; it seemed that she anchored him now. It was an awful time for her, too, with her husband on some distant battlefield while she coped with increasing tensions on the home front. But Lilo had connections that would prove important to Alex and his friends.

Miles away from Munich, it is easy to imagine Sophie's anticipation as the beginning of summer session studies approached. Soon she would stroll along the promenades or cycle down paths of the *Englischer Garten* not far from her brother's apartment in Schwabing. During the final months of compulsory service at Blumberg, Sophie could only fantasize about life in the city. During her six months as a kindergarten teacher, she compensated for losses by immersing herself in the environment's natural beauty. In all, she had spent twelve months in the service of a regime for which she no longer had enthusiasm, but for which she now held contempt.

Here there were no great cathedrals like Munich's *Frauenkirche*, the 15th century Trans-Gothic/Renaissance spectacle. Even though a Protestant, the ritual and sacred spaces of Catholicism held an appeal for her. In Blumberg, though, spirit found home in solitude once again. In her spiritual diary she lamented the scarcity of books from which to gain some solace. Sophie suffered terrible homesickness. For her, there were no concerts. Munich's music halls were far beyond her reach, so for awhile she satisfied her passion for music by writing to faithful Otl, remembering the joy and healing its sweet sounds brought into her life.

One day, when a package arrived, she tore off the postal wrappings, uncovering a book, a gift from Han's friend, Professor Muth. Earlier, when she learned about her brother's mentor, she had taken it upon herself to send him a few apples from the countryside. The book she now held was a thank you from him. Sophie could not believe the old man's generosity to a young woman he had never met.

Finally, the arrival of another spring renewed Sophie and marked the time to bid her farewell to Blumberg. Walking with the girls under her charge, she felt a harmony and fondness had grown between them. Happiness filled her when she thought of leaving on such a positive note. Physically exhausted from endless chores, Sophie packed her belongings and left Blumberg for a month home in Ulm, ready for a new phase in her life. Leaving the solitary life she experienced while fulfilling her National Labor Service, she wrote to her friend, concerned with re-orienting herself into the society of family and friends.

After her respite at home, Sophie finally prepared for the long-awaited departure to the university. She folded the linens and placed them with the baggage already filling up with the skirts and sweaters packed for her trip to Munich. Magdalene joined in, pressing the collars and sleeves of her daughter's blouses. Excitement filled the preparations, but Sophie would miss her mother's attentiveness. During the two years since her high school graduation, there had been many separations from her parents and home, but this time it meant realizing her dreams, not serving the Führer but setting her own course.

She thought about the recent days with Fritz in Freiburg and his warning to be careful. Sophie's fiancé feared her attitudes and her outspokenness could bring trouble, and her questions about securing a duplicator and her request for money for a vague reason, made him fear the worst. He knew how little she tolerated words without action. Did she already know what waited in Munich besides the biology labs and philosophy lectures? When she snapped shut the latches on her suitcase in Ulm, did she lock inside a determination to participate in Hans' plans? Years later, Fritz, and Sophie's sister Elizabeth had a strong suspicion this was so. Then again, there may have been secrets Hans had no intention of sharing when Sophie arrived in Munich.

In a few days, Sophie would celebrate her twenty-first birthday. She could detect the sugary aroma of her mother's gift—a crisp brown cake, an almost miraculous creation when rationing made essential ingredients prized possessions. Next to the birthday confection, Mother propped a bottle of wine for a Munich celebration with Hans.

On the morning of her departure, Sophie combed her long dark hair, once worn short in a boyish cut, and decorated it with a daisy. Loaded down with the necessities of college life, she boarded the train for the trip to Munich. The face of mother may have faded as the figures at the railway station grew smaller and smaller, but the face of her brother grew clearer and more distinct when Sophie reached the central railway station in Munich. The familiar square jaw, the high forehead, the determined look in his eyes—finally Hans and Sophie stood together on the platform.

It was like a dream. Sophie's birthday wine bottle bobbed in the chill waters of the River Isar. Late on that May night, the little gathering in the *Englischer Garten* sang and laughed to the sound of Alex's balalaika. Mother's prized cake

had been devoured and Sophie felt an almost instant camaraderie with the young people Hans had gathered to help celebrate. Earlier at Hans' apartment, they had shared poetry and
discussion, and now music and nature—all that spoke to
Sophie's heart.

Sophie received a warm welcome in Munich. Grateful for
the housing arrangements Hans had made until she could get a
room of her own, she looked forward to the greeting she would
receive at the house in Solln. Once again Carl Muth made his
way through his books and journals to open the door for
another young Scholl. Now it was Sophie's turn to enter the old
journalist's world of the "secret Germany."

# CONSCIENCE

THE DUPLICATOR'S ROTATING DRUM BEAT RHYTHMICALLY, turning and turning, over and over, as the next leaflet fell off the press. The summer days flew by until June was nearly July. Christoph still believed that lofty words would not touch the common people crowding the streets of Germany. Both citizens and university students would need a concrete message, one that embodied more than a conceptual discussion of individuality and conscience. The first leaflet had the feel of a reading evening, the philosophical inquiry of young intellectuals. Language less heavy-handed and simpler might better inspire others to resist the excessive demands and lawlessness of the government.

The voice of the White Rose sought crispness and clarity. Though Christoph prodded for the practical, Alex and Hans continued with a passionate discourse on law and called upon an ancient sage, Lao-tzu, unfamiliar to many of the Volk who had been forbidden to partake of any culture Hitler considered un-German. The voice drew once again from the wellspring of reading that had transformed adolescent minds and hearts. In the Scholls' Ulm apartment, Werner had lined the bookshelf with Lao-tzu, Buddha, Confucius, the Koran, and Sanskrit writings.

As the student-soldiers stuffed the second leaflet into stamped and addressed envelopes, the fledgling White Rose grappled with bridging the gap between intellect and active resistance.

## Concepts of Leaflet of the White Rose II

*The young writers strengthened the voice of the White Rose, speaking more directly to the situation in Germany in 1942. National Socialism, the students accused, was a system whose foundation rested on intentional lies and deception in order to gain power over the people.*

*Next, the finger pointed to those intellectuals who earlier opposed the system but later disappeared. They were a failed leadership. The second leaflet announced the time for thought was past, and the time for gathering a critical mass to liberate the nation was present. The voice railed against the dark cataclysmic state of affairs and cried for enlightenment.*

*Alex and his collaborators set forth the evidence, an indictment for crimes against humanity:*

*For the first time, there was a public statement condemning the mass killing of Jews.*

*And there was more:*

*The handbill reported that boys from the occupied lands were being sent to concentration and labor camps, and the girls were used as prostitutes for the SS.*

*The leaflet wondered why the people did nothing. Their guilt was in their slumber, the voice blamed, because it provided an opportunity for the twisted crooks and criminals in the government to have their way.*

*The authors had not yet finished shaming the desensitized masses
but continued delivering the verdict: Guilty!*

*The second Leaflet of the White Rose concluded by recognizing
that good and evil were in a state of confusion. Words from the Chinese philosopher, Lao-tzu, closed the document along with a postscript that again urged recipients to duplicate the handbill and pass
it on.*

After thumbing through phone directories, selecting
names at random or intentionally for those known as possible
supporters, Alex and Hans contrived a system for mailings. Visits to the post office required careful planning; the threat of
interrogation hung over large quantity stamp purchases, and
bulk mail also could raise suspicion. Small numbers of
envelopes mailed from numerous sites could better deter the
sharp eyes of local watchdogs.

Christoph, like the others, tried to preserve a modicum of
normalcy in daily routines at the Luftwaffe military hospital at
Lake Eib. When home, he devoted himself to Michael, known
as Mischa, and Vincent, two little boys he loved as precious
treasures. In a letter to his half-brother, Dieter, Christoph
related a berry-picking adventure with his sons and their
delight in searching and capturing the sweet fruit. The Reich
could not smother this passion for life.

ONCE AGAIN, SOPHIE SETTLED into a place in the lecture hall where
only a few scattered chairs remained vacant. Students from
many disciplines, though not officially registered for the
course, slipped into the room to audit the class. Willi Graf's
friend had informed him of the professor's reputation. Others,
like Sophie, had come to Munich to study philosophy, and this
teacher did not disappoint their expectations; he may even
have exceeded them.

The slight figure of a man limped to his position facing
the eager students before him. The crowd quieted as Kurt
Huber began his lecture, deliberating each word. The students
strained to decipher his sometimes garbled speech, some not

wanting to miss those subtle jabs at the regime and innuendoes strategically punctuating his delivery. The man had nerve.

The professor stood before the attentive students. For twenty-two years he had been lecturing in philosophy, psychology, and musicology. Life before Hitler had immersed Huber in a research of world music. It was a time when, dressed in a tuxedo, he could sit before a conductor, ready to perform in a concert of Indian music. It was a time when he dared to speak about the richness and diversity of other cultures even as remote as the South Seas.

Distinguished by a productive career, the rise of the Third Reich demanded that he navigate through narrow straits. The regime had hit hard at the university with its *Gleichschaltung*, the program of coordination, which required institutions to align themselves with Nazi thought and goals. But as a philosopher might contemplate, there existed unwritten laws that needed obedience, even in the shadow of a government demanding the surrender of individuality to unanimity.

In 1942, Huber conducted his lectures at the edge of a sea of students, many wearing the swastika. The professor made a firm distinction between serving one's country in the Wehrmacht and serving the Reich. He had heard the whispers of mass atrocities in Poland and the Soviet Union that leaked out by returning soldiers. Later, a student confirmed some reports when confiding what he knew to Huber. The professor was approachable. On one occasion, Hans, Sophie, Christoph, and Alex, after hearing his remarks during a political discussion at a literary evening, became convinced that including him in the Eickemeyer's studio gatherings was a good idea.

After lectures, Sophie frequently returned to her new address at Mandlstrasse 1. She had stayed only a short time at Carl Muth's, but she remained deeply devoted to the gracious, elderly man. Trying to strengthen his health with nutritious gifts, she wrote to her parents asking them to procure scarce food items for him.

In continuing letters to her friend Lisa, Sophie told about the hours of conversation during tea at Muth's. This new world challenged her equilibrium when talk turned to how an individual must act under a dictator. Guarded but attentive, Sophie moved from isolation to immersion in the exciting but complicated life of a university woman. Munich quickly became familiar with Hans' help, and her fondness for her brother grew stronger now that they spent so much time together.

Whether Sophie already had a hand in the composition of the Leaflets of the White Rose, or whether she later became a quiet witness to the mysterious appearance of these messages, she embraced their sentiments.

Sophie had committed herself to acts of non-cooperation during the past winter. Her refusal to contribute warm coats, heavy blankets, or old skis for the soldiers on the Russian front demonstrated her desire to thwart the war effort. When Sophie wrote confiding her actions to Fritz, he lashed out at her, thinking about his comrades who shivered together during the bitter Russian winter. Sophie responded that death was an evil outcome of a war she believed Germany must lose. She did not want to take any action that would promote it.

Sophie felt more resolute than ever to morally oppose the regime that now threatened to throw her own father into prison. Herr Scholl, a financial consultant, had befriended a young secretary at his office. Once in passing conversation she had asked what he thought of the Führer. Without hesitation Robert, mincing no words, called Hitler a curse on the German nation.

The woman, convinced it was her patriotic duty, denounced Scholl.

Once again Gestapo officers invaded the Cathedral Square apartment, rummaging through the rooms searching for incriminating evidence. The secret service police interrogated Robert and then hauled him off to prison where they locked him up for several days, charging him with malicious slander of the Führer. His later release was temporary; the trial would begin some time during Sophie's summer session in Munich. Sophie feared for her father and the sentence that might be imposed on him. His condemnation of Hitler was not out of character, though; it was father who had kept the family aware of political matters, often engaging in black listening, secret listening, turning the radio's reception to forbidden air waves reporting the war's progress. It was Robert who advised his children to consider the war of National Socialism as a sinister force devouring the soul of Germany.

As she adjusted to her life in Munich, her father's safety preyed on Sophie's mind. Within weeks of her arrival, she confided in a letter to her friend Lisa that she sometimes felt overwhelmed with the ideological discussions saturating her. All the talk stirred a desire to put thoughts into deeds.

The question of when Sophie did take action remains unanswered.

Early versions of Sophie's inauguration into the White Rose leaflet campaign painted the following scene:

Imagine Sophie scanning the smudgy print of a handbill, racing over words condemning a regime for robbing its citizens of their free will and paralyzing their spirit. Her eyes sweep over the second and third paragraphs that beg the German people to reclaim their lost individuality. Someone had dared to publish and distribute this rousing message. If Sophie had turned the sheet to read the rest of the appeal, she would have discovered excerpts from the work of Goethe and quotations from Schiller, authors familiar to her.

Perhaps one day, Sophie browsed through books scattered about her brother's room. Sifting through the pages of an old Schiller volume, Sophie might have noted a page with a portion of text underlined—a segment referring to the lawgivers, Lycurgus and Solon.

It would cause her to pause. The underlined text sounded familiar. These same words in Han's book paralleled the quotes in the leaflet she had read. Perhaps it was then she realized that her brother might be the author of the handbill. Certainly she might fear the danger of *Sippenhaft*, clan arrest, especially with her father's recent difficulties with the Gestapo. Whether Sophie's initiation into the secret work happened just this way remains unclear, but it is likely she would worry about the consequences to her family for actions she or her brother might undertake.

ONE BY ONE SEVERAL PEOPLE HANDED OVER COPIES of the second Leaflet of the White Rose to the authorities. They could be arrested for not turning in such forbidden and seditious sounding material; some did not want to take the risk. The Gestapo, agitated by the mysterious appearance of the traitorous leaflets, resolved to snag the perpetrators quickly and put an end to it.

The quest for the best words continued. Christoph lent his criticisms, now joined by Jürgen Wittenstein, another student in the Second Company who helped edit the forthcoming third leaflet. Reflecting back to this time, Lilo remembered a visit to her apartment when the authors asked Christoph for his comment. His verdict: too moderate. Christoph's growing certainty about the necessity of resistance prompted him to confide to his wife that something had to happen. Herta, having no knowledge of her husband's secret work in Munich, felt uneasy.

Quickly, following the second, a third leaflet surfaced that summer.

## Concepts of Leaflet of the White Rose III

*In this leaflet, the voice of the White Rose admitted that a government cannot be all ideas but must develop organically just as the individual human does. The family was recognized as the first social organization having as its basis the harmony of the individual and the common good of the whole. The youths presented the divine order as the highest model to imitate and the goal for which to strive.*

*Without arguing a preferred form of government, the emphasis was placed on performance; what counted was security for the individual and the good of the whole. Speaking in the first person, the voice then asked why, even though citizens of Germany knew the government was evil, they let it take away their basic human and civil rights and could not muster the courage to get rid of it. Again, as in previous handbills, the White Rose warned and prophesied: the worst was yet to come if no action was taken.*

*For the first time, the authors outlined actions that would weaken the hold of the corrupt government—passive resistance. The list was extensive, but the voice reminded the individuals to listen to their*

*own intuition. The young dissidents called upon the people to exercise resistance through what they called sabotage, mainly through non-cooperation, sanctions, and boycott in the following venues:*
   *Armament plants*
   *Public rallies*
   *Science that supported the war*
   *Nazi-sponsored cultural events*
   *Pro-Nazi media*
   *Financial and material support for the government*

*This time the authors concluded by holding up a mirror in the form of Aristotle's work, Politics, in which he defined a tyrannical system as one that subjected citizens to incessant surveillance, and one which set the people against each other under a warrior tyrant. With a final plea for passive resistance, the leaflet closed with its characteristic postscript: Please copy and distribute.*

Not all leaflets ended in the hands of the Gestapo. When Traute read the contents of an envelope pulled from the mailbox, she welcomed its thoughts but puzzled over the references to classical literature, the Goethe and Lao-tzu. The young woman heard echoes of the literary circle at Eickemeyer's studio. She knew: It's one of us. Finally, references in later leaflets led her to Hans. He denied it, not ready to claim authorship. She accepted his silence but took to heart the postscript: Please copy and distribute. She traveled north to home and Hamburg, motivated by a feeling that a network might be forming; she buried a copy of leaflets among her possessions, feeling, perhaps, that something could be done. Months later, she would contact her classmate from high school days, Heinz Kucharski, and his sympathetic circle. Word would spread in the North.

Sophie attended classes during the long, warm, summer days. On Sunday mornings she sipped her coffee and wrote her letters. She still waited for her parents to send her bicycle so she could save money on transportation. Sophie also prayed to God.

One evening brought a new guest into the discussion at the studio. The door opened for Professor Huber who had responded to Hans' invitation. Conversation would now tackle questions raised by philosophers like Kant: Is it morally necessary to do duty for duty's sake? Is the way a person treats others a means to an end or an end in itself? Similar queries absorbed Traute, Willi, Sophie and the others gathered together. After an evening such as this, Alex invited Kurt Huber to gatherings at the Schmorell residence. Huber did not yet know the identity of the White Rose authors who would soon release another statement.

## Concepts of Leaflet of the White Rose IV

*The voice of the White Rose began its fourth leaflet with a summary of recent German military successes and stalemates, noting the dual responses of optimism and pessimism. Alex and Hans warned against excessive optimism because of the price in human lives. Again, as in the second leaflet, the youths pointed to a confusion of good and evil, but this time they targeted Hitler directly.*

*The fourth leaflet took a metaphysical turn, naming Hitler as Satan's accomplice, and National Socialism as the servant of the Antichrist. The voice of the White Rose made an appeal to Christians to reject this evil. It reminded the readers that saints and prophets had appeared throughout history to reconnect people with the higher order of God. This spiritual message was supported with lines from Ecclesiastes 4—then an excerpt from Novalis.*

*Hans and Alex added to the text by acknowledging the need for military action to take down National Socialism, but what they asked of their readers was to recognize guilt and to reclaim the spirit of the nation. Approaching the conclusion, the leaflet demanded punishment for Hitler and others who had committed crimes against humanity.*

*The authors assured the readers that their message was not connected to any foreign power, and that the names of recipients were not written down anywhere.*

*The students' words shouted that the White Rose represented the conscience of the people and would not be silenced.*

In a matter of sixteen days, from late June into July 1942, the voice of the White Rose had launched its own blitzkrieg. If Sophie had not participated from the start with the conception, production, and distribution of the publications, or if she had not accidentally discovered her brother's authorship shortly after her arrival in Munich, then with the distribution of the fourth leaflet, another scenario has been suggested that may have happened like this: During summer session at the university, students filtered out of lecture halls, some taking a break before another would begin. One of those students, Traute Lafrenz, handed Sophie Scholl a handbill reading, "Leaflet of the White Rose IV." Hans was there, too, not looking the least suspicious. Then he moved closer, leaning over Sophie's shoulder to read the document. She wondered what the White Rose could mean. Later in the week when Sophie asked Hans to speculate as to the author, he warned her not to ask because it was safer for the writer to remain unknown. If this is actually what happened, then it probably was not long before Sophie learned the truth. Wherever and however she learned that truth, she joined her brother and Alex with conviction.

Sophie had been in Munich barely three months. When the summer semester ended in July, the Reich thrust her into more compulsory work in a munitions factory just outside her hometown of Ulm. She attempted to convince the Students' Administration to assign her as a service girl to a family or as a receptionist in a doctor's office; she hoped for something other than the weapons factory. Sophie had asked her military friends to resist shooting anyone when they went into the army, and now the regime forced her to devote the next two months to the Führer's munitions assembly lines. Like other women students, she would not be allowed to return for the winter term of 1942–43 if she failed to complete the service she dreaded.

Hans and Alex had to move quickly when the rumors proved to be true. They had just twenty-four hours before their departure from Munich. Rather than gathering supplies and setting up shop for another leaflet production, they hurried to dismantle and hide the evidence, securing the paper, stencils, ink, and duplicating machine. Their campaign had gained some momentum, but now the pulsating grumble of the mimeograph machine ceased. Tomorrow the Wehrmacht planned their transport to the Russian front.

In the Second Student Company barracks, soldiers gathered supplies and a few personal items for departure according to standard regulations. Willi Graf tucked his diary into his pack—the entries, though sparse, kept a log of his journeys in and out of his student-soldier life. After three months in Munich, the Wehrmacht once again pushed him into Russia. Having suffered the dust, heat, and insects of a Russian summer, he knew what to expect. Once again, the men assembled for roll call: Graf, Schmorell, Scholl, Wittenstein, Furtwängler…On and on a voice called out the names, accounting for the entire student medic group. But tonight Willi planned to go to Eickemeyer's for a farewell party hastily organized when the orders for the company's assignment proved imminent.

Because he was in the Air Force and the head of a family, Christoph would not be shipping out with his friends. Yet, he continued to fight his own internal battles. His brother Dieter remembered Christoph's moments of turbulence during 1942. His friends were going off to the battlefront, but he believed Germany's war must be doomed and the Nazis defeated. Later, Christoph confided to Dieter that his frustration was reaching a breaking point.

Dieter worried what dangerous response his brother might contrive.

On a summer night in late July, tea, wine, and little cakes greeted Christoph and the other guests as they drifted into Eickemeyer's studio once more. The architect himself was present this evening to bid farewell to the young soldiers scheduled to begin the long journey the next day. His agitation had increased in recent days, and his impatience with so many of his countrymen, puppets of Hitler's regime, diminished his sympathies for the ravages of war they experienced.

Tonight his studio provided a friendly retreat for these young people whom he may have considered the last gasp of human creativity. The blackout curtains covering the windows of the studio could not, however, hide the anxieties of another guest, Kurt Huber. The professor found a place to sit down, exhausted, not from physical effort, but from the heavy mental burdens he bore as he witnessed years of Germany's cultural history strangled by its own government. Countless works of art had been declared degenerate, sold, or destroyed. Galleries, like the Old National Gallery in Berlin, pock-marked from endless air raids, might never see the masterpieces of the German Romantic artists again. It was as if the barren trees and church ruins of Casper David Friedrich's "Abbey in an Oak Forest" mirrored the ruin of the traditional cultural centers of the nation.

Nearly fifteen guests arrived and mingled in casual conversations. Willi, Alex, Christoph, Sophie, Traute, Hans, and others chatted about literature, music, and philosophy as they emptied their glasses and refilled them again. But lighter talk drifted on to more pressing matters. The professor took the lead in a debate about active and passive resistance. Not all present, including the professor, knew that the authors of the White Rose leaflets gathered with them in the very room where they met that evening. The professor continued his arguments. He could not imagine the intellectual community taking to the streets and marching in public protest. Maybe they could appeal to non-cooperation. Maybe they just had to wait. He could entertain fantasies, however, of sabotage, or even of the assassination of Hitler.

The sound of those ideas hung thick in the air. Why even Hans had passed some time in a monastery to study the idea of tyrannicide, and there he settled it with his conscience. Guests milled about the room as the idea of recruitment came into focus. The group needed more people to help spread dissident attitudes and call for passive resistance.

During the party, a high school student, Hans Hirzel, stopped to say good-bye to Hans. He had read copies of the White Rose leaflet, and he had a strong suspicion that he knew the author. Yet, he said nothing. Hans Scholl, his thoughts half still in Munich and half already on the train into the vast Russian plains, pulled Hirzel aside to give the youngster eighty marks. He was to find and purchase a duplicating machine. Hirzel stared at the money in his hand. He would hear from Sophie when they were both in Ulm.

As the evening progressed, the young soldiers moved closer and closer to a dawn that could be their last in Munich. Hopefully, they would return, but they were not naïve; they knew the risks.

Huber asked Hans to keep a record of his impressions of Russia. As the professor began to make his round of good-byes, Christoph stepped forward, ready to escort him through the darkness to the streetcar stop. The teacher limped alongside Christoph's steady gait—out to the streets, exposed to the threat of the incessant Allied bombing raids, caught in a contradiction: protect the homeland and destroy the common enemy, Adolf Hitler.

# Chapter Ten

# DEPARTURES

SOPHIE CUPPED A WHITE FLOWER IN HER RIGHT HAND. A book bag hung on the spiked iron fence separating her from the small band of soldiers. In these farewell moments at the *Ostbahnhaf*, her eyes focused on Hans and their friends; her ears absorbed snatches of their conversation.

The Wehrmacht had ordered the soldiers to the railway platform at seven in the morning. Finally on board, Willi searched for a seat in the assigned section for his unit, glad that this time he would be with his friends Alex, Hans, and other student medics like Jürgen Wittenstein and Hubert Furtwängler. He had packed the essentials—apples and some books. Unlike his last, lonely assignment to Russia, intelligent conversation would carry him through the long hours of waiting and travel to the Eastern front. There was so much he was leaving behind. Recently, thoughts of his sister Mathilde's wedding occupied him. He hoped for her good fortune. The future was difficult to think about sometimes, especially with so many interruptions in lectures, laboratories, clinical work, and one's personal life.

By eleven on that Thursday morning July 23, 1942,

sounds of departure reverberated throughout the *Ostbahnhof* as the train rumbled out of the station and headed for Warsaw. Sophie was alone now, but for days she would remember this morning. When she wrote once again to her friend Lisa, she told her of the separation's deep imprint, awestruck by the strong bonds she had formed in such a short time in Munich. Sophie held those parting moments close, hoping for the safe return of her brother and new friends.

The transport clanged and rocked over the Danube, speeding through Zwickau, Dresden, and onto Gorlitz. For all of Friday and Saturday the broad expanse of land opened itself to Willi and Alex and the others. Hans lounged comfortably in a compartment as the train rolled steadily along rails stretching through the Polish landscape. Alex lit his pipe and leaned forward as he read a book. Occasionally the train clattered over a bridge, and sometimes the rocking and swaying of the car lulled them into a quiet sleep. If monotony took over, the friends amused themselves with games. If it got too hot, they could open the vent of the vast window and gaze for hours at the bucolic countryside dotted with farmhouses capped by thatched roofs. Breezes from the birch woods and forest lands gave them some relief.

Hans' uniform jacket hung from a hook along the wall behind him. He rolled up the sleeves of his shirt, unbuttoned his collar, and relaxed into the train's rhythms. The endless plains and expansive sky lured him into thoughts of men and women steadfast in their praise and love of this beautiful land. The lovely countryside, the open fields, and the changing colors of sunset and moonlight made him think of the Polish prisoners in Germany, those wrenched from this place, their homeland. The train snaked closer and closer to Warsaw.

AN UPHEAVAL TORE THROUGH WARSAW during that sultry summer week. Beggars littered the muddy, stench-filled streets; some propped up against the ten-foot stone walls that for two years had isolated the Jews from the 'Aryan section' of the city. News of another train's departure ripped through the Warsaw Ghetto. Confused voices shouted to each other in the streets—

something about a transport traveling to the East for resettle-ment. The authorities assured the so-called settlers they could each pack forty pounds of luggage and food supplies for three days. Panic seized some. Others fell prey to the lies. Still, some sensed the unpredictable realities of the Nazi reign of terror. Only workers in the German factories and workshops or those holding some position of authority could now expect to remain in the ghetto. Their families would stay as well.

Within the Warsaw Ghetto stood the Pawiak prison. Fif-teen-year-old internee, Mary Berg, opened her diary and wrote, "July 22, 1942. Today the ghetto had a bloody Wednes-day." What had been feared had come to pass—violence in the streets and deportations.

A man wearing a ragged jacket dragged himself through the street and into the doorway of his quarters. Another trudged along in shoes cobbled with scraps of discarded leather. A motionless body lay bundled in a blanket. These were to be among the first 'settlers' the police cleared from the streets and herded to the assembly gate, the *Umschlagplatz* on Stawki Street.

A string of sixty wagons formed a train alongside the ghetto's northern end. It would be traveling north and west out of Warsaw tomorrow at four in the afternoon, shuttling 6,000 Jews the sixty miles to *Treblinka*. Tomorrow, children who lay exhausted and withered upon filthy mattresses were likely to be among the one hundred crammed into one of the sixty waiting rail wagons. Grown men would fill the daily deportation quota by kidnapping little ones roaming the streets and carting them to the train. Their cries for their mothers haunted the ghetto.

Mary Berg peered from her prison window and watched as adults rushed into Korczak's children's home and minutes later left, each grasping the hand of a little child. She heard the prison guards' whispers of random shootings and beatings whenever someone stepped out of line. Gunshots. Screams. Resisters crumbled under the brute force of those Mary called "beasts." These youths, not much older than she, trained in cru-elty.

Chaos.

Beggars. Children. Volunteers for deportation, malnour-
ished families bribed with the promise of a kilogram of bread
and work, swelled the crowd gathering at the *Umschlagplatz*. A
thin question rose from the crowd: How far is it to the farms
and the fields that await our labor? The train ground out of
Warsaw; sixty wagons would return empty each day, seven
days a week for seven weeks.

On a July Thursday in 1942, six thousand Jews, packed
into cattle cars, departed from the ghetto. White armbands
labeled with a blue Star of David identified the settlers: preg-
nant women, children, intellectuals, grandmothers, and ex-sol-
diers wearing the rags of once proud uniforms. Old men
wrapped cloths around their heads to symbolize the ritual
beards forcibly shaven or burned from their faces. They sizzled
inside the windowless containers, some straining for relief
offered by air drizzling through cracks between the wagons'
planks. They passed through the countryside with its birches
and farmhouses with thatched roofs. No toilets, no water,
nowhere to sit, no air.

A railway worker heard the gunshots in the distance,
heard the roar of the approaching train as it neared *Treblinka*.
Most did not realize death waited for them a short walk away.
The Nazis had a name for this street, *"Himmelfahrstrasse,"* the
"Street to Heaven."

Willi, Hans, and Alex arrived in Warsaw during the first
days of the massive deportation of Jews. It is not clear what
they witnessed. They were free to explore Warsaw on the layover. Late Sunday afternoon Willi and his friends ventured into
the heart of the city. His diary entry condensed the experience
in a simple but profound word—misery. Had they seen what
lay on the other side of the wall? That summer night, Willi
wilted into deep sleep.

The next day the young medics returned to the city to
roam the streets and sit for awhile at the Blue Goose. Money
was dwindling, so as Willi later recorded, they rationed their
drinks. The men garnered little satisfaction from the stopover in
Warsaw. Willi may have seen, once again, that which he had
hoped never to witness.

Hunger ravaged the city. The Third Reich enforced an official formula for daily rations: 2000 calories for Germans, 699 calories to Poles, and 184 calories for each of the Jews in the ghetto. Dark bread and watery soup were often useless to men, women, and children too weak to pick it up and bring it to their mouths.

By Tuesday, July 28th, the German medics packed their baggage and waited most of the evening for the hospital train that would detour through the pouring rain to Russia where they would tend to sick and dying German soldiers. A few weeks later, Hans, Alex, Willi, and Hubert sent a message to Professor Huber at Ludwig-Maximilians, mentioning the deep impact of the city and the ghetto.

The train pulled away from the city where beyond the copse and the birch, and after the pink skies had drained to gray and melted into darkness, shadows would stalk the forests along the rail lines. Camouflaged by night, gangs of Soviet prisoners of war would flee from the Nazis. Jewish refugees, not deceived by the empty promises of resettlement, would risk treachery at the hands of rapists. Women and children would hide while men foraged for food to fill their aching stomachs. Others would join the partisans, finding there a measure of release for their outrage.

In this July of 1942, a few Jews would resist by escaping to the Aryan side. A Jewish underground fomented. At every turn, a Nazi manhunt threatened.

The medics' train disappeared into the East, leaving behind the seething ghetto. Tomorrow would condemn another six thousand Jews; the doors of the wagons bolted once again. Faces would appear behind grates of barbed wire, and the moans and cries for water and for a doctor would evaporate in the heat of the oven-like transports.

Mary Berg, the Jewish girl in the ghetto prison, thanked the little American flag pin she wore each day. Her mother's American citizenship saved her from the cruelties of the streets and the probability of deportation. She hoped to reach freedom through a prisoner exchange, but for now, in the days when German soldiers on their way to the Russian front passed through the streets of Warsaw, she bore witness to the life behind the ghetto walls, wondering why the world did not come to the rescue.

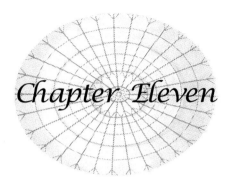

# Chapter Eleven

# BRUTALITY

WILLI GRAF AND HIS COMPANIONS MOVED PAWNS across the chess board as the train slipped through the borders of Lithuania. Alex, Hans, Willi, and the German army pounded towards the oil wells in the Caucases. Stalingrad lay in the ferocious path of the Wehrmacht, and the possibility that Russia could lose the Volga River was, for the Soviets, a grim reality.

From Warsaw the medics advanced eastward to Vyaz'ma. Willi turned pages of the *Bridge over San Luis Rey*, reading for long stretches. When the train stopped briefly at Wilna, there was time enough for Willi to capture some sun and relax on the grass. It had been almost a full week since leaving Munich. Then the transport pressed ahead again. Signs of war scattered along the rails as talk of partisans and evidence of their work came into view.

By Sunday morning, August 2, the soldiers had arrived in Vyaz'ma. According to Adolf Hitler, they were now in the land of the Russian sub-human beasts. During the brief layover before moving onto Gzhatsk, closer to the front, Hans and the others visited a Russian church. The experience so moved him that in his Russian diary, he later wrote a lengthy poetic reflection whose words and phrases attempted to capture the experience. The icons, the light, the simple, strong devotion of the peasants—all he observed strengthened his own hope for a spiritual fire that would renew human souls.

Hans had a different understanding of Hitler's "beasts."

The troops pulled out of Vyaz'ma and positioned themselves in Gzhatsk, less than one hundred miles west of Moscow where the Führer's planned blitzkrieg had failed. Moscow had not collapsed as Hitler prophesied. The Russian's resilient fighting spirit fortified them against the Wehrmacht's onslaught.

Hans raised the glass to his lips and let the schnapps slide down his throat. He drank not to forget but to surrender to laughter. Alex joked with their peasant companions who lived and worked near the German encampment. They, in turn, rallied around the German soldier who spoke their language and curried tunes from the balalaika. At night under the big Russian sky, Alex's nickname, "Schurik" suited him better than ever. Hans recorded moments like these in his diary.

In Gzhatsk for just a few weeks, Russia's soul intoxicated the young Germans. Long before their combat internship, images of Russia, rising from the spirit of Rainer Maria Rilke, drew them into a cosmic view of the poet's adopted homeland. Russia appeared colored in metaphysical hues. They savored the nights they danced with Russian girls and prisoners of war. When Willi got lost in a lively evening, as he would when he was a youngster at home, his reserve would loosen, disappointed if it broke up too soon. Alex, animated by his desire to bridge the gap between the German soldiers and the folks of his maternal ancestry, reveled in such evenings.

In more subdued moments, they drank tea and listened to the songs of a Russian worker in their camp. Willi's diary began to fill with sentiments of love for Russia's land and people. Russian fever overtook them. Some nights Alex and Hans and their comrades slept soundly in their dugouts. Some days crawled by in idleness as the rains soaked their encampment at Gzhatsk. The young men pulled themselves away from the restless hours, venturing out for long walks in the forests turning golden with the change of season. The contrast of good and evil proved stark. At night Russian artillery shells strafed Gzhatsk. There was talk of partisans. Trains splintered and iron bent at the saboteurs' hands in the occupied lands. Paratroopers floated down behind the German lines.

HANS WORRIED ABOUT HIS FATHER. When a letter arrived from his mother in mid-August, he knew he had to talk with his brother Werner stationed in the same sector just a few miles away. He mounted a horse, charging over the landscape that on a mellow day had hypnotized him with flowers lining the railroad, fields of grasses, and flocks of jackdaws flying overhead. When he reached Werner's camp, Hans delivered the disturbing news that the Reich had imposed a prison sentence on their father. Magdalene wanted her boys to sign a petition for clemency, hoping that such a letter from two sons at the front would impress the authorities and set her husband free. When Hans left Werner to his orderly duties, he wound his way back to his dugout near Gzhatsk. Hans' diary noted his initial reluctance to beg for mercy.

Hans settled on a wooden crate, lit a candle, and followed its flame as his thoughts turned to his father. He pictured Robert isolated in a narrow cell. Fury had turned to indignation to resignation in the days since he had another letter from mother. When her sons eventually complied and submitted official pleas on behalf of their father, Magdalene felt relieved, though the outcome still remained uncertain.

Hans' turmoil turned him to his books, yet even there he found little comfort. The beauty of Goethe's works now seemed somewhat detached from the suffering world. Nights filled with restless dreams and daylight with wanderings in the woods. It was a time and a place for inner demons to surface. Death visited the camp daily, though it rested far-off from the front.

Alex and Hans had walked just one hundred meters from their dugout when they saw the corpse of a Russian, once a whole person, now scattered parts exposed to the elements. They dug a ditch and covered the dead man. The medics tapped nails into wood, fashioning a Russian cross to place at the grave's head.

Bombs shattered the beautiful land. The Russians torched their own villages and black smoke billowed from their sacrificed homes. Nothing should be handed over to the invading Germans.

In the flat grassy plains, Russian soldiers, raising their arms in surrender, staggered across fields of tall grass.

In the Wolf's Lair in Eastern Prussia, Hitler plotted the next move for Operation Barbarossa. He was still confident that: "We only have to kick in the door and the whole rotten structure will come crashing down." Others had their doubts.

The men in the Second Student Company heard reports of the Russian advances to the north and west of their encampment. But other enemies prowled closer to the makeshift field hospitals or concealed themselves in dugouts among the soldiers, the prisoners of war, the Russian girls, and other local peasants. Many could not withstand the armies of fleas or lice leaving tracks of red spots, fever, and the severe headaches of typhus. Others could not resist the assault of an infection that set fire to intestines and beset the victim with intense diarrhea—the foe called dysentery. Every day the medics armed themselves for combat with infectious diseases.

Bacteria struck Alex. Overnight his body fired like a furnace, exposing him to the possibility of further assault: weak pulse, restlessness, confusion. His friends worried about their own strength to fight diphtheria. The threat of contagion forced Alex into isolation.

In early September, orders issued to Willi and Hubert sent them packing gear again. Horses clip-clopped along roads, drawing ambulances behind them and assembling the transfer of troops to Staroye and to the 461st regiment. Willi learned he had to walk to meet the first battalion.

Hans sank into melancholy while Willi and Hubert forged closer to the front with the infantry, and Alex battled his fever. In mid-September Hans crouched in the dugout by candlelight and scrawled in his notebook, harboring thoughts of escape, but wondering where he would go. Some days he sat along the river bank, his companion a Russian fisherman. Other days he stopped off at Werner's camp. Still others, he fled to the plains making his getaway on horseback. He temporarily escaped into the quiet moments and the exhilaration of the gallop across the fields. He wrote to his parents three days before his twenty-fourth birthday telling them that nature's beauty could tempt one not to acknowledge ugly truths.

Alex felt stronger as September leaned into October. He avoided giving any more blood as the medics often did; he needed to rebuild his resistance if he was to go back to his work at the surgical station. Time in Russia, the place of his other life, would soon run out. Thoughts shifted toward Munich as word spread that the Second Student Company might soon evacuate the camp. Hans' periods of self-absorption began to turn around as he redirected his thoughts outward. A return to Munich would mean re-establishing the White Rose leaflet campaign left behind. He and Alex talked.

Fall began to ease into winter in late October. The Wehrmacht's successes against the Red Army had rallied the morale of the Germans during July and August. But the Führer underestimated the Soviets' intention to make a last stand at Stalingrad. Now as late autumn threatened winter snowfall, Soviet logistics confounded the Germans and stymied their advance.

The long days of being stuck in foxholes and mud were over for the student medics. Reunited at Vyaz'ma, Willi, Alex, Hans, Hubert, and others in their group settled in the sun. Alex, especially, needed to rest. Each took a turn accounting for his activities during their separation. On October 31st orders were given to report for delousing. Instead, they agreed to escape to town where they bought a samovar for brewing hot black tea during the long journey back to Munich.

Through the first days of November, the train vanished from Russia and slipped into Brest. When the transport pulled into the station, they heard a terrible racket; a German guard bullied a Russian prisoner of war. The medics taunted the soldiers and offered their cigarettes to the prisoners. The train pulled out before any disciplinary action could be taken against them. They were lucky. They could have been court-martialed, thrown into prison, or even put to death for aiding the enemy. It had happened.

A German officer in the Wehrmacht had photographs of a soldier whose compassion during the invasion of Yugoslavia had cost him dearly. The soldier's name was Joseph Schultz. Schultz and his unit of the 714th Wehrmacht division marched into a village where fire blazed in the hollow shells of what had been peasants' homes. Foot soldiers hurled torches into doorways of buildings—everything exploded in dense black smoke. Schultz and his small band of soldiers were commanded to a site where villagers lined up, leaning against a wall of hay. Some blindfolded captives gripped the hand of another. The executioners positioned themselves parallel to their targets. The commander shouted the order—all but Schultz raised a weapon. He was called to follow the others. Schultz refused. Ordered forward, stripped of his helmet and weapon, the German soldier was led to a gap in the line-up. He stared at his comrades as he leaned against the dry wisps of straw. The firing squad raised their rifles and carried out the commander's orders. In a moment, Schultz lay dead among the slaughtered villagers.

The stopover in Brest could have turned out very differently for Alex, Willi, and Hans. Hans had taken such risks before by giving tobacco to a Jewish laborer and offering his food rations to a Jewish girl forced to work along the railroad tracks. If either of these captives had attempted to escape and hide, they would have been hunted down with machine guns or chased by armored vehicles. They could get away for awhile, but later could freeze and starve in the forest. A laborer could be sent to a construction site, handed a shovel, and commanded to dig anti-tank ditches. Others could stand in water, straining under the effort to drain a marsh. All along the railroad, on the front lines, throughout the occupied areas in the East, prisoners sweat or froze while digging artillery dugouts. Hitler valued these people only for the labor they could provide for the New Order.

What Eickemeyer had reported to Hans months earlier,

the young German soldiers may have seen for themselves. They left the East where labor camps turned to death camps, and laborers dug their own graves. Alex, Hans, and Willi could linger to smoke a cigar or take a few puffs on a cigarette before tossing it aside, but extending such a luxury to the enemy was considered a sign of weakness. The Third Reich's warlord preached to his commanders, "Close your hearts to pity. Be brutal. Obtain what is theirs. Be harsh."

In four days the soldiers arrived in Munich. They had a different plan.

# Chapter Twelve

# RESISTANCE

SOPHIE LIKED THE RUSSIAN WOMEN working on the munitions factory assembly line. The gaudy earrings these women wore fascinated her; they seemed to match their easy attitude despite the hardships these laborers suffered. The woman next to her did not have to smile or try to be helpful to a German co-worker, but Sophie felt her warmth, her generous spirit. It was reminiscent of Schurik—spontaneous and open like the broad Russian plains.

Each workday the clock ticked long minutes as ten hours dragged on. Waiting for the right moment, when other business distracted her supervisor, Sophie helped the women sabotage the weapons they assembled. She refused to obey one of Hitler's countless slogans, *"Guns Before Butter,"* by offering scraps of food to the Polish and Russian conscripts whom the Nazis uprooted from occupied lands. The Germans collected seven and a half million people as slaves for the Third Reich. Some, forced to walk to Germany, journeyed with possessions packed across their shoulders. Some picked their way bare-footed over rocky roads and winding terrain to the final desti-nation—wherever the Nazis needed labor.

The war machine wielded a power far greater than Sophie could combat alone, and she squirmed from the rub on her conscience. She wrote to Lisa confessing how terrible she felt about the munitions work and the war it promoted.

Sophie hated the racket of the machinery, the boredom, and the piercing siren signaling the end of the day. Yet, without these annoyances, she felt she would not have gained a perspective that she admitted had altered her understanding of the conditions of war. Working side-by-side with the prisoners gave her a greater awareness of their misfortune at the hands of the German government.

After work hours, the family apartment on Cathedral Square was not the same haven it had been. Sophie worried when she noticed her mother weakening from her battle with heart disease. It had been a consolation to Magdalene that her boys, Hans and Werner, had contact with each other at the Russian front, but the strain of her husband's imprisonment caused her great anguish. The household trembled with the ordeal of separation from Father.

On a lingering summer evening while her brothers were still in Russia, Sophie headed toward the prison where the Reich had locked Robert in a small cell. She carried her flute. Once near the prison walls, she stopped, raised the woodwind to her lips and let her fingers dance along the octaves. No orchestra accompanied her; the simple solitary voice of the reed filtered into the shadows of the departing day like a bird taking flight. Sophie's notes, those of an old German protest song, *Die Gedanken Sind Frei* drifted skyward. "I think as I please/And this gives me great pleasure."

The Scholl women had gathered together, adding messages to the single letter Robert could receive every two weeks. Sophie scribbled reassurances that she sent thoughts to keep her father company. They often waited long for a reply; the regime allowed Robert to respond only occasionally.

Father's familiar sounds had disappeared from the apartment. He was among the many Germans who took the risk of listening to forbidden broadcasts despite dire consequences, sometimes as severe as death, for tuning to the BBC. Robert's warning that a sinister voice waged a battle against the soul of Germany and humanity, lingered in his absence. Sophie studied the map of Europe without him.

By the end of September, she fought the depression of those dark days, seeking even a trace of light. With work service completed, she could plan an excursion into the forest and drench herself in nature's healing energies. During his imprisonment, Father's office was maintained with the help of a gentleman named Eugene Grimminger with whom the family had regular contact. With management worries settled, she could dream about a getaway. She envisioned an isolated farmhouse, a place to disappear to for awhile—or so she thought. A message from Munich arrived: Carl Muth's house in Solln had been damaged in an air raid. Quickly, Sophie scratched her outing plans and returned to Munich to help him.

Sophie came to loathe the cult of violence—its specter hung in her thoughts and meditations. At night, the drone overhead often warned Munich that bombs would soon target and crumble public buildings and private homes. Citizens ran for cover, cringing in air raid shelters. Suspicions surfaced that the tides of war had turned against Germany.

Sophie's letters confronted Fritz with thoughts of good and evil, heaven, hell, and salvation. She did not hold back, even though she knew her fiancé did not share all her attitudes. She puzzled over philosophical questions, trying to untangle her emotions; again she fled to Augustine. She prayed to God, even when she felt God was obscured from her vision and understanding. How could autumn colors blaze in beauty with such terror in the world? Sophie longed for a letter from Fritz. She could not stop herself from racing to the mailbox each day, worrying for his safety but telling herself he was just too lazy to write. To her German officer, she issued challenges not only about faith and strength but also the meaning of victory. She pressed him to think about the future and a career after the war. She laughed, too, when she sang Christmas carols in October, weaving sprigs of fir into a handmade Advent wreath she would send to him in Russia. Sophie would wait for his letters.

Waiting was a condition familiar to Sophie. It was a welcome surprise when the authorities granted her father an early release from prison. The family had not expected Robert home until December, and now he returned in the late days of October. His sons' written pleas had done the job. Sophie's wish, that her father could breathe fresh air and enjoy a beautiful sky, came to pass. Hans wrote to his parents in anticipation of the family's reunion. Werner hoped he, too, could soon be with all of them in Ulm.

It was nearly November, and Hans' approaching arrival triggered a jumble of emotions. Once again in Ulm, Sophie had accustomed herself to the rhythms of home, enjoying moments of playing piano by candlelight. During autumn she renewed her correspondence with Otl , stirring up the intellectual conversations and spirit of the *Windlicht*. Sophie's strong connection to Otl consoled her.

She waited again as she had before, quietly, thoughtfully, and alone. She wrote to Fritz in early November 1942, announcing Hans' impending return and hinting that important work lay ahead.

After the train ground to a halt in Munich, Alex, Hans, and Willi left the station and headed home. A brief furlough reunited them to the people and places they loved, to all that sustained them, molded, trained, and educated them. An embrace and a handshake would draw them back to the intimacies of family life. The Scholl household would fill with conversation, catching up on the events of the past three and a half months. Alex could share his impressions of Russia with his father in Harlaching. Willi would talk again with his sisters, Anneliese and Mathilde. And all three medics could look forward to visits from Christoph.

November also meant organizing a return to the university and classes at the end of the month. They could resume conversations with Professor Huber and visit with Carl Muth. The upcoming Christmas season promised new beginnings. The candles on the Scholls' Advent wreath measured the days in a sacred circle of evergreens, a focus for prayer, meditation, and celebration.

Russian harmonies began to fade as the men returned to

the Bach Choir and to Handel's *Messiah*. But the imprint of Nazi atrocities in occupied lands pushed Alex, Hans, and other friends of the secret Germany, out of the shadows and into the business discussed in hushed tones during July's farewell party.

It was almost ten years since Adolf Hitler seized control of their homeland, and their generation grew from childhood to young adulthood under the tutelage of a social order rewarding them for supreme obedience to a single warlord. Many fell in line; others, who did not, set out on the dangerous path of resistance. The return from Russia signaled the escalation of another offensive. The voices of the White Rose reached a new pitch as they prepared to join others to form a more organized underground.

Alex had no reason to mistrust Lilo when she arranged for Alex and Hans to meet her friend Falk Harnack in Chemnitz. The Harnack circle, an academic German family, included Falk's older brother Arvid and his American-born and bred sister-in-law, Mildred, who risked helping with the escape of German Jews. Other political dissidents knew the Harnacks would gamble their own safety to assist them. They already courageously undertook the documentation of Nazi atrocities committed on the front. They also dared to provide military and economic intelligence to Washington and Moscow. Later the Nazis would call the group that congregated around them the "Red Orchestra," labeling them Soviet spies and categorizing their leftist ideology as communist.

When Hans and Alex arrived in Chemnitz, a city close to the Czech border, a young corporal from a reserve infantry met them, suggesting they move their conversation to a certain hotel. They knew Falk Harnack had connections to Berlin, the city that had become the point of in-gathering for splinter resistance groups. They hoped the meeting with Falk would link the small band of Munich dissidents to a more organized resistance. Alex and Hans sought strength in numbers.

Falk Harnack had advice for the young medics from Munich where he also had attended lectures a few years earlier. In the early 30's, his experiences with student demonstrations and leafleting had taught him some useful strategies. The years since then had taken him into the Wehrmacht and also into the classroom and theater as both professor and actor. He knew how to draw attention to ideas in ways that would attract large audiences. He counseled the two visitors from Munich. Once again they heard: Simplify the message in your leaflets. Streamline and clarify the important points in language the common person will understand. The poetry and philosophical references of the summer leaflets will not reach the masses that need to be moved.

They would meet Falk again in Munich.

With each week that Operation Barbarossa bogged down and German casualties soared, the impetus for another leaflet intensified. Russian winter besieged German soldiers left behind in the dugouts, villages, and flatlands of the Russian steppes. Temperatures plunged and snows whipped against their faces. Hitler refused to heed the warnings of his advisors, convinced that he alone should formulate the military strategies in Russia. Doubt rippled through Germany, and the Reich responded with intense propaganda. The volume turned up on the slogans, assaulting both troops and the populace. Hitler stood steadfast as he proclaimed: "We are barbarians. We want to be barbarians. It is an honorable title."

At home in Ulm, Sophie's mailbox ritual continued until one day it rewarded her with an envelope from Fritz. In a moment, fear and relief converged as her eyes raced over his message. Fritz battled isolation and never-ending anxieties at the front. She understood but wished that merely thinking of her would keep him going. Her reply mirrored her own attempts to bear the burdens of war's separation—pray.

Other matters gnawed at Sophie, and she needed to discuss them with Fritz. Father had lost his job since his trouble with the Reich; they now labeled him unreliable. She wondered how he would manage to support two college students and maintain his household at the same time. The family, already forced by rationing to be frugal, would now have to find new ways to make ends meet. Sophie remembered Fritz's generous offer of financial assistance to the family, and now she alerted him to their predicament.

Sophie sent an appeal for money. Because Fritz was a soldier at the front, she might not have committed to writing the real reason for her request. Her mission was a secret, so Sophie simply stated that she needed money. With Fritz's 1,000 marks and Willi Graf's 50 mark donation, Sophie began to tally the available funds for purchasing duplication and distribution supplies. Sophie added a 200 mark contribution from Manfred Eickemeyer to the growing account. Additional money would help troubles with postage. She was familiar with the problems of sending letters and packages in the mail, but in the past had overcome some obstacles with Werner's help. He would send postage to her from the APO, and she would use them to send packages to him. Maybe Fritz could get her some envelopes, too. Sophie knew the leaflet campaign would tax her nerve, imagination, and the treasury which she managed. She relied on her usual unruffled composure to steer through the purchase of hundreds of stamps.

Paper presented a special challenge, not only in cost but also in availability. Even when Hans had scribbled through his last days in Russia, his letters grew shorter and shorter because paper was so precious. Now they would need thousands of sheets to carry out their plan.

# *Chapter Thirteen*

# *CIRCULATION*

Hans and Alex met the fifty-year-old man on an inconspicuous train-loading platform in Stuttgart. It was a city enclosed by forest-covered hills, a city where houses climbed up the slopes and some folks hiked steep lanes to their doorsteps. The young men exchanged cautious words with Eugene Grimminger, Robert Scholl's friend with whom Sophie and Inge had become acquainted at their father's office. When Grimminger learned of the leaflet campaign and listened to their request for financial support, his own disgust with the regime pressed him to agree. He knew well the injustices of the system; his wife was Jewish. They spoke for awhile and then parted. Days later a check for 500 RM arrived.

In early December 1942, Alex, Hans, Christoph, and Willi Graf discussed possible collaboration with other student groups throughout Germany. Willi's attendance at the Eickemeyer studio evenings and his experiences with Alex and Hans in Russia had confirmed him as a member of the inner circle.

Traute had already driven north to Hamburg, where inland waters run to the sea. It was a city of ports and docks and quays, home to a university, a place where non-conformist students concealed their talk in obscure bookstores. During a stay in her home city, she slipped White Rose leaflets to sympathizers. They approved. Collaboration began.

Sophie traveled to Stuttgart, a city of two universities and academies devoted to fine arts and music. She met with a girlfriend from her days of kindergarten teacher-training. Sophie invited Susanne to Munich for a gathering at Eickemeyer's studio, but Susanne declined, offering the explanation that she was too busy with her music. They talked. Susanne doubted that getting rid of Hitler would save Germany; one of his henchmen would fill the vacuum. Sophie challenged that something had to be done. Sophie slid envelopes into several different mailboxes before she left Stuttgart.

Hans, intense, committed, impulsive; Alex, open and unrestrained; Sophie, deliberate, reflective, determined; Christoph, cautious yet convinced; and Willi, once reluctant but now ready to take the plunge—all prepared to move forward.

When the group settled in for another evening to discuss outreach or to structure a security system or to formulate emergency escape plans, the Reich would view them as enemies of the people. Their bid for freedom would be defined as democratic individualism, the antithesis of National Socialism. Their gathering would be labeled a political debate strictly forbidden by the state.

In their absence from Munich, most had come to the difficult realization: Germany had to lose the war to get rid of Hitler. Now their efforts could merge with fragments of resistance from communist to liberal to conservative to military. Though they held the common desire to free Germany from a cruel despot, their diverse strategies and visions could weaken the outcome. Would a dissident Army officer conspire with a communist? Could they unite to end the ten years of treachery that had caused so much human suffering?

Willi turned in the gateway at Franz-Josef -Strasse 13 and walked the path to the Garden House, meeting Hans before their trip to Professor Huber's house in Gräfelfing. Their visit would present an opportunity. That winter afternoon, Hans was ready to take the next step with Huber. He turned the conversation to the current dangerous situation, arguing that the people needed to hear a point of view different from the Reich's reporting. Hans ventured the idea of a leaflet campaign as a counteraction, one to raise citizen consciousness.

Hans waited and Willi listened for Kurt Huber's response.

Questions followed. Huber asked the visiting students to consider the operation's risks, reasonableness, logistics, and effectiveness in reaching their goals. He had his doubts.

Huber had encouraged his students to think and had even taken jabs at Reich leadership, delighting students with his logic and sometimes acid remarks. Active resistance, away from the relative safety of the lectern, would bring his criticism to another threshold.

Willi and Hans left Huber's house without a commitment.

For two years Hans had frequented the L. Werner Bookshop, stopping in as much for the conversation as for the reading material. The manager of the store, Josef Söhngen, had become a friend and confidante, and Hans had been pleased to receive a letter from him while in Russia. But mostly they asked and answered questions of a religious and philosophical nature, each taking a turn. In July the bookseller had received four leaflets of the White Rose, and because Hans felt sure of Söhngen's disaffection for the regime, he admitted he had authored them. Josef agreed that should an emergency arise, the duplicator and the publication materials could be hidden in the basement there at Maximilianplatz 13. Now that plans moved into high gear, Hans visited once again, setting forth the campaign's new direction. Some days Hans would retreat to a chair and its company to recollect himself. Josef let him be.

At the end of December the group disbanded once again for a short holiday break. During the Christmas season, some German families gathered around radios undercover, turning their dials to VOA, the Voice of America. They listened to theologian Paul Tillich's challenge to release themselves from servitude to the Reich.

Christoph wrote a Christmas letter to his brother Dieter

with a message for peace. He knew this year the celebration would be a quiet one.

Sophie relished the comforts and attention showered upon her by her parents and sisters at home. She did not seem to mind sacrificing her independence for a taste of the security she felt there during the holiday. Sophie and Hans, assigned to the little room upstairs, suddenly were children again, warm and safe on a cold winter's night. Snow on the roof insulated them and muffled the terrors of the past year. Silence. And then, just as they may have shared midnight stories years ago, they now raised midnight questions. In the darkness the dialogue emerged: What does God's omnipotence mean? Is God capable of good only? Is God unable to be evil? The night turned silent again.

During his Christmas furlough Willi Graf searched for old friends from *Neudeutschland* days when holiday treks meant adventure more than they meant dangerous business. He set out from his home city of Saarbrücken with its imposing baroque buildings, some now shaken from bombing raids, and others already crumbled in a heap. He always worried about his family's safety; they would have worried for his had they known the nature of his wanderings.

Willi would report that his friend Willi Bollinger, a medical officer in Saarbrücken, could help make traveling easier for couriers delivering handbills. He would provide Graf with army railroad tickets, passes, or forged leave papers. With Heinz Bollinger, Willi shared thoughts religious and political, convinced they still held the common attitudes of their former school days. Willi would call upon the Bollinger brothers again.

Upon their return to Munich, Hans and Sophie shared the same address at Franz- Josef- Strasse 13, their two rooms tucked tightly in the Garden House back building. Some mornings the artist, William Geyer, would join them for breakfast when he was in Munich working on a stained glass project. Hans had arranged for Geyer to use the Eickemeyer studio since it provided good light and had sleeping space, though no cooking facilities. The Ulm artist tolerated the work week separations from his large family, appreciative of the Scholls' arrangement. With Geyer there, Hans may likewise have appreciated the easier access to the studio and its basement. The artist raised no suspicion; his criticism of the regime made him a comfortable addition to the evening discussion circle.

TROUBLE ERUPTED ON JANUARY 13, 1943. When Gauleiter Giesler of Munich stood at the podium, ready to address the university student body, the hushed audience waited. Young men, many student-soldiers, packed the auditorium, and women students filled the balconies. They had obeyed the order to attend this celebration of the university's anniversary, some unwillingly. Few, like Sophie Scholl, did not attend. Gauleiter Giesler's voice bellowed propaganda slogans: duty, leadership, new horizons. Then, he turned on the women, condemning them for wasting time in study, for hiding from their true obligations to the Reich. Were they trying to avoid work service? They should be laboring in the munitions factories. They should be bearing children for the Führer. Then, with blatant sarcasm he asked: Were unattractive women unable to get men to impregnate them? If so, Giesler promised to provide men who would honor Hitler and accommodate the girls. Jeers and shouts burst forth from the women, some rising and rushing toward the exit, there stopped by a wall of Gestapo. Some men heckled and whistled; chaos exploded as they rushed in defense of the women. Giesler did not finish his speech. The celebration ended in shambles.

The leaflet organizers saw promise in the news of this upheaval. General student unrest could till the soil for their cause.

Sophie cautiously approached the postal clerk behind the counter, feigning business as usual when she knew this transaction could land her in prison. She tried to purchase as many stamps as she could without causing the clerk to have a second thought or a second look. She handed over the money, slipped the stamps in her bag, and left quickly. Different routes and different locations prevented her from becoming a familiar or suspicious face.

Not long after their trip to Gräfelfing, the professor

joined Hans, Willi, Sophie and Traute for tea at Franz-Josef-Strasse. Willi later reported that on that January evening, the men alone briefly heard Hans read aloud an incomplete draft of the fifth leaflet, with Huber offering editorial comment. Then the men joined the women for tea with no further discussion.

The hypnotic spin of the machine spit out copy after copy of the fifth leaflet refined by Professor Huber's critique. With donations from Grimminger, an efficient machine cranked out more than just hundreds of copies, piling them in thick stacks. Just half the length of the previous four, the January 1943 handbill no longer flashed a *"Leaflet of the White Rose"* banner. Rather, it proclaimed itself, *"Leaflet of the Resistance."* The students had come to identify themselves as part of a larger collaboration. When one in the group tired, another took over, churning the drum. Ink seeped through the type carved into the waxy stencils, printing the words on each sheet of paper.

## Concepts of Leaflet of the Resistance

### (The fifth handbill)

*Retreats in the East and the threat of massive US build-up foreshadowed the fall of Germany, the fifth leaflet asserted. The apocalyptic tone warned of an impending invasion and punishment for a criminal leader and nation that followed blindly. The authors foretold a future when Germans would be scorned by humanity for their actions and indifference.*

*A series of imperatives, one quickly following the other, created a sense of immediacy in the authors' arguments. The language urged a retreat from bystanderism and called citizens to action.*

*The final words did not reach into the classical past as in the earlier White Rose leaflets, but projected a future free from militarism and devoted to an alternative federal state and world cooperation. The leaflet concluded by holding out the possibilities for the attainment of basic human rights. Even the postscript sounded more assured, commanding rather than asking for support and distribution of the message.*

Hans casually entered a phone booth, flipped to a page in the directory, and left a flyer in view. Later, someone would enter the same booth to make a phone call, consult the directory, and discover the paper, reading its challenge to disassociate from National Socialism. Would the caller turn in the paper? Leave it? Or, would the reader take it and pass it on to someone else?

In Munich, a young soldier boarded a train bound for Berlin. He carried a suitcase. He placed the valise on a storage rack in a passenger compartment. He did not take a seat but wandered away, hoping the authorities would not stop to examine his leave papers. A military policeman approached him. The officer brushed past. Hours dragged by before the train screeched to a halt at its destination. The young man retrieved the suitcase and exited into the city where he posted the leaflets.

During the third week of January, Willi wove his way through the heart of the Rhineland, hoping to gather support and distributors for the copy of the fifth leaflet he carried with him. He traveled through Cologne, the ancient cornerstone of its famed Gothic cathedral threatened by Hitler's war, and on to Bonn, a city straddling the Rhine and home of Beethoven and a university. He pretended to be organizing a fencing tournament, setting up participants, and scheduling Bonn vs. Munich, but his secret purpose was recruitment. From Bonn to Freiberg to Ulm, he sought his friend Dr. Heinz Bollinger, finally meeting him in Ulm and handing over the *Leaflet of the Resistance.* Open to a connection with the Munich group, Heinz Bollinger knew that in Freiburg, the university had secretly grown its own core of resistance. He would deliver the leaflet.

It was the duty of German citizens to report Willi's political activities to the Reich. Police patrolled the streets, but they could not be everywhere. Good citizens were expected to monitor neighbors and strangers for the nation's security. Those who had listened and not reported him could be imprisoned for years. Willi's recruitment efforts constituted high treason according to the Reich criminal code. The Bollingers knew the risks.

Some citizens who picked up mail on a winter morning

in Ulm, Augsburg, Freiburg, Cologne, Berlin, Stuttgart, Salzburg, Vienna, or Linz, read the *Leaflet of the Resistance*. Alex, Jürgen, Hans, Sophie, Willie, and Traute traveled, duplicators moved, and the number of distributors expanded.

Sophie transported a suitcase to Ulm. Relieved to have come this far without incident, she lifted her bag off the train. She handed over contraband leaflets to high schooler Hans Hirzel who had recruited a few friends to help; one was named Franz Müller. Years later Müller recalled an earlier first encounter with the White Rose message. At a farewell evening before his National Labor Service obligation, a few friends passed around a bottle of wine. An hour later a friend said he had something to share. It was the *White Rose Leaflet IV*. Franz remembered being touched by the message, but feeling the need to know more. Another in the group objected, saying that he would not join in resistance with a former Hitler Youth, namely, Hans Scholl.

In January 1943, Hirzel approached with a plan for distributing the fifth leaflet *"Leaflet of the Resistance."* Franz started addressing envelopes, working behind the organ of the Martin Luther Church in Ulm. He worked in fear. In retrospect, Müller wondered who was closer to death—the boys on the Russian front or the boys hiding in the church. Hans Hirzel did not limit his work to Ulm, but with his sister, carried mail to Stuttgart.

Approximately 11 o'clock on one of January's last nights, Alex, Hans, Willi, and Sophie gathered in the Garden House for their special mission. Willi picked up a briefcase filled with leaflets and left, walking to Franz-Josef-Strasse and Ludwigstrasse. He entered a streetcar and traveled toward his assigned section of the city in the direction of the River Isar. Darkness hid him and the others as they scattered leaflets in Munich neighborhoods. Willi headed home two hours later.

Copies of *Leaflet of the Resistance* crowded the desk of the Reich officer. He picked one up and read. As the situation in Russia slid into catastrophe for the Sixth Army, the Volk could lose faith in the Führer and be tempted by these sparks of resistance. A special committee of investigation formed to track down the perpetrators.

IN THE WINTER OF 1943, THE SIXTH ARMY FROZE in Central Russia. Horses sank up to their bellies in snowdrifts. Wind knocked soldiers off their feet and hurled them across the icy flatlands. Sophie's Fritz could not keep his hands warm and dry. They froze, thawed, and froze again. The spaces between the body tissues began to crystallize. Several fingers turned numb and stiff like wood, pink skin turning to gray-blue. Day and night the expectation of capture or death shadowed him.

In the prisoner of war camps, starvation drove crazed Russians to cannibalism. The commanders of the Wehrmacht begged for permission to surrender, desperate to save lives of the remaining soldiers. Hitler refused. Surrender was forbidden. The Sixth Army must stand their ground to the "last man and the last round."

The landlady at Franz-Joseph-Strasse 13 fled her apartment for the countryside and an escape from the escalating bombing raids over Munich. The students kept going, sometimes dodging the air raids, guarding the safety and security of the mimeograph, and planning other storage space if Eickemeyer's should get hit. At any time Alex, Willi, or Christoph might show up at Hans' and Sophie's apartment.

The door opened and Christoph stood at the threshold. He could not stay long, just an hour or so. Christoph, now the father of a baby daughter, talked about his wife Herta and her hospitalization for post-natal sepsis. His mixture of joy and concern had not prevented him from keeping contact. Christoph weighed risks carefully for himself and his friends, but now he prepared to make moves that earlier he might not have dared.

For some time Herta had a vague notion of group discussions in Munich, and she had recognized her husband's distress over the debacle unfolding on the Russian front. One Sunday, in the kitchen of their little apartment, Herta prepared the family meal when she noticed her husband scribbling something. Curious, she asked what he was doing. Evading an explanation, Christoph picked up the paper and left the room.

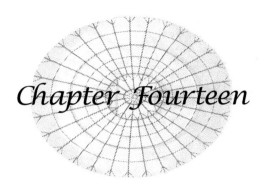

# Chapter Fourteen

# WRITING ON THE WALL

COUNTING LEAFLETS, SOME WRINKLED and others neatly folded, the Gestapo measured the growing stack—three inches, five inches, seven, ten inches. In two days about thirteen hundred copies of the *Leaflets of the Resistance, A Call to All Germans* turned up in the intense high treason investigation. Rounds of communication sped from the Reich Security to the Gestapo and back. City police in Munich, Stuttgart, Augsburg, Nuremberg, and other places where citizens had handed over the seditious material, either due to commitment or fear, received high alert notices. Uniformed officers scoured maps, marking sites where the papers had appeared or tracking envelope postmarks. Crime lab experts studied the pink or blue colors of the papers and the clarity of each letter typed. A watermark, a manufacturer, a retailer, all served as clues inching them closer and closer to the perpetrator.

During the last weeks of January, the students' studio conversations grew deeper, and the circle grew larger with the presence of Theodor Haecker and the entrance of Christoph's father-in-law, Harald Dohrn. Religion and theology mixed with debates and visions of a future German state after the war.

Meanwhile, the Gestapo kept watch for suspicious activities, spying on individuals known to have oppositional views or a previous arrest record for seditious crimes. Others patrolled railway stations or confiscated customer lists from retailers selling paper.

During those same days, quiet talk passed among the dissidents: The deteriorating situation in Russia doomed German troops there. Christoph Probst placed a blank sheet before him and thoughts spilled over.

### Concepts of Christoph Probst's draft, "Stalingrad!"

*Christoph Probst condemned Hitler's sacrifice of German soldiers' lives, and his refusal to retreat or surrender in the face of an inevitable defeat. Christoph argued unconditional surrender meant life, not death and affirmed that such surrender to the Allies would not destroy the people but would rid them of a corrupt regime. He wrote that the hate that drove the persecution of the Jews was the hand that robbed citizens of their freedoms. He warned that the same hubris slaughtering human beings in the occupied lands could also turn on German citizens unless they withdrew their support of the war.*

*Christoph concluded with a plea to citizens for action.*

The Reich would say such words and actions betrayed the troops. They could chide him with reminders that the National Socialist system had generously supported his medical studies and his wife and children. But increased bombing of northern cities set alarmed German citizens, women and children now refugees, flooding south where Allied raids were less intense. Even in the South, Christoph Probst, stationed in Innsbruck with his Luftwaffe unit, kept his family in Leermoos, a less likely Allied target. Soon Christoph handed over the draft of his thoughts to Hans Scholl.

In Munich experts continued to measure the size of the envelopes and analyze their texture, grade, and design. Updates to the state police in Vienna and Frankfurt traveled the wires. Investigators puzzled over questions of when, tracing the hours the leaflets appeared on city streets, in phone booths, or parked cars.

In late January, two Hitler Youths in Ulm denounced a young man whom they knew involved himself in seditious activity. They had heard from him directly about leaflets of resistance he helped to print and distribute. A connection to Sophie Scholl threatened.

Sophie hung up the phone, thrilled with the news. Fritz had evacuated from Stalingrad—alive. In the first days of February, she would follow his progress, anxious for word as he transferred from one hospital to another where he slowly recovered from the amputation of two fingers. Sophie dared to think there was a future after the war.

On February 3, 1943, the German citizens crowded around radios for a "special bulletin." Beethoven's Fifth Symphony flooded the words they were not surprised to hear, yet loath to believe:

The Battle for Stalingrad was over. The Germans were defeated.

The Red Army had succeeded in encircling the Germans; 400,000 soldiers of the Wehrmacht had been deployed in the Russian campaign, and less than 100,000 survived. Hitler's plan, fashioned in the isolation of the Wolf's Lair, was a catastrophe laid bare. Now German prisoners of war, blankets strapped over their shoulders, fought the bitter cold, shuffling along on icy ground. The Volk's confidence wavered during the dark, somber days when the newspapers thickened with obituaries.

Funeral marches and lowered flags marked official days of national mourning. Even while Goebbels heated up the propagandist rhetoric to rally the staggering populace, a sense of betrayal shrouded the Volk. Once, sure of their invincibility, a feeling of vulnerability now settled over them. The Allied bombing raids shattered their nerves and their homes daily. The Führer never visited the ruins to stand in the rubble of a once beautiful city.

Just days after the fall of Stalingrad, Sophie left Munich

for Ulm to care for her sick mother. During this time, Fritz's mother relayed messages about her son's condition. The empty mailbox still disappointed Sophie daily. The Hartnagel family, though, proved far more fortunate than hundreds of thousands of German families whose sons did not return from Russia.Whenever Sophie visited Ulm she took the opportunity to move forward with the cause. She sought out her Ulm connections and continued the secret work. Then, with family matters in Ulm settled, she returned to the university.

In Munich, when Alex finished cutting templates, he and Hans grabbed green paint and brushes and plunged into midnight's darkness. They slipped through the shadows of Ludwigstrasse to the shrine of Hitler's putsch. Dipping the brush, smearing the stencil, they left behind a banner, "Freedom." They plastered walls with "Down With Hitler." They struck X's through dozens of swastikas. Tomorrow, students at the university would see another point of view.

The next day Russian prisoners of war scrubbed the stubborn giant letters: "Freedom." The "Down with Hitler" splashed on stone walls outraged some passers-by but delighted others who tired of being Hitler's slaves. Students on their way to lecture muffled their comments and their surprise; someone could be watching their response.

Crowds hurried to Professor Huber's lecture. In the wake of Hitler's travesty in Russia, grief crushed the teacher. Graffiti would not change the course of the war, but a few well-chosen words could spark a stronger resistance to the whims of the madman who was destroying the Wehrmacht. When Hans Scholl invited the professor to his apartment for a meeting in early February, he agreed. Falk Harnack arrived in Munich to visit with Lilo. He too would be at that meeting.

Tragedy had struck Falk's family since the conversation with Hans and Alex in Chemnitz. Three days before Christmas, the Reich charged his brother Arvid with treason and hung him from a meat hook—death by slow strangulation. Arvid left a farewell letter thanking his family for their love and support. Now Falk's American sister-in-law, Mildred, languished in a prison cell, passing her last days translating poetry. Her sentence to six years of hard labor had been withdrawn; her fate later sealed at the guillotine.

In the past, the Reich upheld the image of solidarity by hiding news about resisters. But with the collective grief after Stalingrad, the Führer tightened the noose, and press reports of executions appeared more frequently. Let those who did not remain loyal beware.

The group meeting in the Scholls' apartment understood that individual resistance proved useless, and collaboration of small pockets of dissidents promised the beginning of a consolidated attack on National Socialism and its leaders. During their discussion, a clash of ideologies, even among those unified in their hatred of the regime, became very clear. The conversation turned to visions of Germany after the war. Falk's idea of a planned economy, a type of Communism promulgating a highly socialized society, provoked strong opposition from the professor. To Huber it smacked of Bolshevism.

The professor grew agitated. How could he cooperate with a communist? Alex, Willi, and Hans, however, entertained compromise for the sake of an immediate coalition with one imperative: Get rid of Hitler.

With Professor Huber in their circle, the group could not dodge weighty ethical questions. It was men like Huber who had dedicated their lives to getting students to think, despite obstacles he encountered from the university's single-minded governing body. He wanted to know how resistance could be carried out without threatening the Wehrmacht and its soldiers. He opposed the current regime's distorted leadership, not the army. This quandary drove a wedge between him and the students.

The discussion at Franz-Josef-Strasse created dissension but also an opportunity for Hans. Falk Harnack would arrange a meeting with Dietrich Bonhoeffer in late February. Even if he didn't embrace Falk's theories, Hans accepted his connections. A meeting with Bonhoeffer would mean ties with a man who had become impatient with the German Christian Church's reluctance to confront National Socialism's inhumanity. Bonhoeffer, a Lutheran minister, was a founding member of the Confessing

Church dedicated to remaining free from Nazism. The regime banned him from preaching and publishing, but his opposition persisted. Faced with questions of morality, he made difficult choices. He joined the German Military Intelligence, knowing he would use his contacts with foreigners for the resistance effort. Even he had come to terms with the possibility of assassination. A connection with Bonhoeffer would join the Munich group to a potentially powerful resistance.

Individuals scattered around Germany were ready, some to duplicate or spread the sixth leaflet. This time Professor Huber composed the text. The Reich expected the professor to be diligent in fostering devotion to the Führer, preparing his students to sacrifice themselves in the regime's battles. The professor, instead, poured out a protest against the decade of violence crushing Germany's spirit. The student collaborators argued over his inclusion of sentiments that supported the Wehrmacht. Huber fretted, but Hans had his way. The students dropped the line and disappeared once again to grind out several thousand copies of the sixth leaflet.

### Concepts of Fellow Fighters of the Resistance! Also known as "Students!" (The sixth handbill)

*The author mourned the dead and maimed at Stalingrad and placed the blame squarely on Hitler's shoulders. The professor and his collaborators hurled the question: How much more? They demanded redress for stolen human rights. Speaking particularly in the name of youth, the leaflet computed the injurious effect of the incessant propaganda upon youths' intellectual progress. Appalled by the Gauleiter's recent attack on the status of university women, the leaflet praised those who stood to defend them. The message commanded its readers to get out of any activity or organization that threatened true education and open inquiry. In moving, powerful language, the voice censured the Reich's distortion of honor's meaning and sent forth a final plea for restoration of Germany's integrity. This leaflet was specifically aimed at students, rallying them to take a stand.*

next day's actions could be clarified if reliable answers could be found to these open questions.

William Geyer, the artist, continued his treks to and from Ulm, having spent most mid-weeks sharing breakfast and sometimes another meal with the Scholls. He later reported hearing Sophie say the evening of February 17th that many deaths had come to those fighting for the regime and perhaps lives would be lost opposing it.

Thursday morning, February 18, 1943, Hans and Sophie prepared to leave the apartment at Franz-Josef-Strasse 13. A suitcase and a briefcase holding approximately eighteen hundred copies of the sixth leaflet passed their final inspection. Sophie carried a key to Eickemeyer's studio. Christoph's written comments for future publication hid in Hans' pocket. At approximately 10:30, they picked up the bags and left. As they had many times before, they walked the streets of Schwabing, hoping they would give the appearance of just another pair of students hurrying towards the university.

Not long after their departure, Otl arrived at the doorstep of the apartment. He was on leave from the Russian front and just a short while in Munich. He had come to Hans and Sophie's as planned during last night's phone conversation. Otl left when the Scholls did not answer, but he intended to return later.

No envelopes or night's darkness shielded the Scholls this morning.

Sophie and Hans needed to arrive before classes dismissed, crowding the hallways and atrium of Ludwig-Maximilians. Two figures, recognized as Traute and Willi, were leaving early for a psychiatry clinic in another part of the city. They delayed just a moment for a quick hello and a questioning look from Traute when she saw the suitcase. After Willi and Traute disappeared towards a streetcar, the Scholls moved forward. Without hesitation they scrambled through corridors, dropping bundles of leaflets and edging toward classrooms on the second level.

Just as quickly, they slid down the stairs towards the exit but stopped abruptly when they discovered a few remaining

leaflets in the suitcase. Gliding up the stairway once again,
Sophie or Hans or both, spilled papers from the balcony, and a
rain of handbills fluttered into the open spaces of the *Lichthof.*
Now the two could flee and not return. But when they
saw a figure coming toward them, Sophie darted into a room,
hiding the key to Eickemeyer's studio in an upholstered chair.
The custodian, Jacob Schmid, cried out: You're under arrest.
The brother and sister waited.

In a second, confusion swallowed the streams of students
rushing into the corridors; some bent to pick up the papers, and
others ignored them. The hallways hummed with questions as
the exits locked. No one was permitted to leave. Jacob Schmid
pulled Hans and Sophie to the administration office, and the
Gestapo immediately took action. It was only then Hans
attempted to slide Christoph's draft out of his pocket, trying to
shred it to indistinguishable pieces before the investigators
could get their hands on it. Alert officers caught him in the act
and gathered up the remnants.

For hours, students remained in lock down; small numbers were allowed to leave periodically throughout the afternoon. In the crowd, Professor Huber looked on, his worst fears
confirmed. As the Gestapo jostled their way through the mob,
students stared at the two suspects escorted to the door. Hans
saw Gisela's face and shouted a message for Alex. Outside, a
curious crowd milled about the university grounds. Alex stood
among them. Was he there by chance or by design? As the captives sped away, Alex knew he must warn Willi.

Investigators rushed to the Scholl apartment at Franz-
Josef-Strasse13 where they tore through the place, overturning
books, canvassing drawers, and collecting stray envelopes,
large quantities of stamps, a typewriter, and other paraphernal-
ia construed as part of a leaflet production and distribution
operation. Returning for the scheduled lunch appointment
with his friends, a confused Otl fell into the Gestapo's snare; he
did not know what had transpired. He would not be the only
arrival at the Garden House that afternoon. Gisela Shertling,
Hans' current love interest, showed up, too. The police
detained the young woman. Unlike Otl, she knew the Scholls'

involvement with the leaflet campaign, and she had witnessed the morning's upheaval at the university.

The search continued as officers scooped up stray notes and letters, among them a handwritten correspondence from Christoph Probst. Later, at Gestapo headquarters, close examination of the script uncovered a match to the handwriting on the scraps of paper Hans had tried to destroy.

Traute, kept her distance on Franz-Josef-Strasse, avoiding the fate of Otl and Gisela, ready to warn any others who might approach the Scholls' rooms. She had parted with Willi after the lecture at the psychiatry clinic on Nussbaum Strasse.

In the future, Willi Graf would offer as an explanation to investigators, the following course of events: When the phone rang, he heard an alarmed Alex telling him to be at a specific Schwabing street corner within the next half hour. At 3:45 Willi arrived. Alex broke the news that two students had been taken into custody at Ludwig-Maximilians. They found a phone booth and decided to try Hans' number. Someone picked up the phone; an unfamiliar man's voice answered at the other end. Willi and Alex sensed danger; they knew they could be next. Fleeing would mean they would be AWOL, and Willi argued this would trigger a military pursuit in addition to the Gestapo. The two men parted.

(MOSAIC AT THE ENTRY TO THE GROSSER HÖRSAAL, AUDITORIUM MAXI-MUM, LMU, 2003) "She would have preferred to be registering at the university in Munich to study biology and philosophy where Hans studied medicine as a student-soldier. That would have to wait; the Third Reich harbored other plans for ambitious, intelligent, young people like Sophie."

(LICHTHOF, LMU 2003) "The stairs, the hallways, the balconies, and the statuary of King Ludwig and Prince Leopold swirled around me—all pieces of the tragic drama that unfolded at this site on February 18, 1943."

(LICHTHOF, LMU 2003) "Light filtered through the eye of the glass-domed ceiling, illuminating the empty spaces of the cavernous atrium, filling its balconies and casting shadows in its archways."

(LMU 2003) "Without hesitation they scrambled through corridors, dropping bundles of leaflets and edging toward classrooms on the second level."

( LMU 2003) "In a second, confusion swallowed the streams of students rushing into the corridors; some bent to pick up the papers, and others ignored them."

(SIDEWALK AT ENTRY TO LMU 2003) "Thousands of leaflets were reproduced, and the Royal Air Force scattered them, sending them floating onto German soil."

(SIGN NEAR LMU 2003) "I recognized the universal language of teachers willing to be open and approachable to their students. It seemed appropriate to be standing near the street sign reading 'Professor Huber Platz'."

(BANNER, CRAILSHEIM, GERMANY 2003) "As a member of the UNESCO Associated Schools Project, a network of schools committed to the ideals of human rights, democracy, and intercultural understanding, the Geschwister-Scholl-Schule not only re-membered the fragments of a painful past but labored to re-member the splintered humanity of the present."

(SITE OF THE FORMER JEWISH SYNAGOGUE, CRAILSHEIM, GERMANY 2003) "Red geraniums and black-eyed Susans surrounded a small monument carved with the Star of David and a simple historical plaque that serves to remind those who would notice: Never Forget. Frau Scharr pointed to the words and translated," Love your neighbor."

# Chapter Fifteen

# FOR FREEDOM

Two OFFICERS CLIMBED THE STAIRS to a second floor apartment at Mandl Strasse 1. At 10 PM, the landlady unlocked the door to Willi and Anneliese Graf's apartment and waited. Neither brother nor sister was at home. The Gestapo sifted through papers, hunting for any evidence pointing to the seditious leaflets. A few envelopes and a few sheets of stationery showed up, nothing that could be construed as aiding the enemy or demoralizing the troops. But the men did not leave the apartment. At midnight, Willi and his twenty-two-year-old sister returned to their rooms and walked into the hands of the officers. They marshaled Willi and his sister Anneliese from the building and marched them to a waiting vehicle. The Gestapo had followed their orders, the apprehension of another suspected student graffiti artist.

Willi grasped his sister's hand as they hung together in the car, but they remained speechless; a word between them might provoke the vigilant Gestapo officers. Doors slammed shut, engines ground over, and the driver pulled away, wheeling them through city streets and braking to a halt at Wittelsbach Palace. Anneliese let go of her brother's hand as the escort pulled her from him. Guards locked them in separate cells on different levels of the Gestapo Investigation Prison.

Wittelsbach now housed several youths associated with the resistance leaflets, each left alone to grapple with the meaning of this detention for themselves and for their families. Already Anneliese, though not a member of the inner core of the White Rose, had been implicated simply because she was Willi's sister. Interrogations had already begun and the list of names grew longer.

When the young soldiers of the Second Student Company assembled for roll call, no one dared cover for an absent friend. In the past Jürgen Wittenstein may have shouted a "Here!" for a missing Willi Graf or Hans Scholl, but today their absence was a stark consequence of the recent upheaval at the university. The Wehrmacht unit was placed under quarantine as the investigations began. Jürgen sensed his commander's hunch that he too had been involved in resistance actions, but the officer preferred to overlook his suspicion rather than have another of his men hauled off by the Gestapo. Extreme caution must be exercised, and Wittenstein considered secrecy a highest priority. Any item remotely related to questioning the Reich had to be concealed. He too had taken risks that required fanatical cover up.

Roll call intensified: Schmorell—Alexander Schmorell. Silence answered.

WHEN ALEX STOOD IN THE DOORWAY OF LILO'S apartment, his race for safety had begun. He stepped inside, shutting out the Gestapo's pursuit. Immediately he must lose his identity and take on another. Lilo had connections, and by Friday an authentic-looking Yugoslav passport bore Schurik's picture. She also arranged forged travel papers.

Gestapo activity heightened in public places throughout Munich. Men and women handed over their papers for inspection, forced to wait while the officers scrutinized the documents. When "Man Wanted" posters appeared on poles, windows, doors of the railway station, and other public venues in Munich, Alex's imminent departure grew more urgent. The

Gestapo prowled the depots, hoping to grab the fugitive Schmorell if he should try to escape the city. A student who could defy the Reich as he had and then successfully make a get-away, would fracture the image of the Volk's solidarity and weaken the regime's power to curb dissidence. For the Nazis there could be no opposition from the populace without stern and swift recrimination.

Lilo urged Alex: Get out now. A delay is a flirtation with arrest. The new pants and shirt, a complete change of clothing, could help camouflage his identity. Alex needed to draw from all the imagination and inventiveness he could muster to devise his flight. He would need to depend upon his Russian connections to gain sympathizers who might protect him. Maybe he could find his way to a camp and pose as a prisoner of war. Perhaps he could flee to the mountains and break through to Switzerland.

Almost two days had passed since the Scholls' and Grafs' detention. Alex slid out of Munich and on to Innsbruck, the traditional junction in the road, a stopover nestled on the trail from Germany to Italy and Switzerland through passes threading their way between lofty mountains. Alex gambled on the crossroad's strategic position to gain access to an escape route.

The streets of Innsbruck curled through the city where tombs of emperors and war heroes rested within the walls of its magnificent churches. It had been almost five years since Germany annexed this city, a mosaic of museums, university life, and ancient battlefields. In February 1943, air raid damage toppled the city's picturesque image, leaving mounds of rubble. Alex hoped his arrangement to meet with a contact would materialize. He tried to keep himself as inconspicuous as possible until the woman arrived. His anticipation grew stronger and uncertainty crept over him as the appointed meeting hour passed. Finally, he realized that waiting any longer was useless; the plan to disappear into the Soviet POW camp had failed.

Now what was he to do? He would have to keep moving. The "Man Wanted" poster shadowed him, turning up at the very places he sought refuge. For a while a Russian helped him hide in a health resort, but someone spotted him. Again he fled.

IN HIS CELL, HANS strained to catch the daylight and a view of the sky—some picture that could transport him from this container illuminated by an artificial light, one that was to burn continuously throughout his imprisonment. Interrogators did not want to lose their captives to suicide before maneuvering them towards self-incrimination and pushing for the disclosure of others. Both brother and sister were given a roommate, an assigned bodyguard. Hans' companion remembers him softly reciting lines of poetry. Sophie could not know whether her cellmate, Else Gebel, a prisoner herself, might be planted there to extract condemning remarks made in casual conversation. She needed to proceed with caution.

For the remainder of Thursday and throughout Friday the investigation hammered Sophie. Inside a room with blinds or shades drawn, one could become disoriented, unable to distinguish day and night.

The Gestapo intended, as with most interrogations, to secure a confession. Often that did not come easily, and the inquisitors would employ psychological and physical coercion. Robert Mohr encountered a self-possessed college girl, gentle in demeanor, soft-voiced yet words spoken with conviction. Known to be somewhat restrained with his investigative procedures, reports suggest he modified his examination further because of the impact of Sophie's personality. He also was the father of a soldier.

The young girl identified herself: Sophia Magdalena Scholl, a Lutheran girl born on May 9, 1921, of parents and grandparents of pure German blood. A short biography followed, one that could not adequately explain what brought her to this moment: Her siblings, her parents, her schooldays, the BDM days, the Arbitur, the work service and the war service, her teacher training, and the summer session at Ludwig-Maximilians.

Sophie did not hide her estrangement from the youth movement or the fact that her attitudes differed from her friend and brother's current girlfriend, Gisela Schertling, who favored National Socialism. When the names Willi Graf and Alex

Schmorell surfaced, she admitted they too were not disposed to National Socialism, but she insisted the men merely socialized as fellow students and friends of her brother—sharing wine, music, and the like.

As Mohr threw more pointed questions her way, Sophie could not buckle under the stress but needed to shoot back with reasonable explanations. Typewriters, stamps, mail—just as she made it through one, another question challenged her resolve. The typewriter was for essays and for Hans' letter writing to their brother Werner who also served in the Wehrmacht.

Perhaps Mohr leaned forward and modulated his voice, beckoning Sophie to recount the events of the morning at the university. Perhaps he leaned back, folding his arms across his chest and demanded she explain the empty suitcase. Investigators knew how to manipulate a suspect, how to rattle nerves one moment and offer a sympathetic tone the next. Sophie steeled herself in order to keep her balance. She was on her way to catch a train to Ulm, but needed first to meet Gisela at the university to cancel their lunch date. The empty suitcase was to be filled with clean laundry at home in Ulm.

Hour after hour Mohr coaxed: Tell us all you know.

Sophie insisted she had nothing to do with the leaflets, altering the morning's events to support her denial: She suggested that when she and Hans arrived at Ludwig-Maximilians-University, the leaflets were already there. She offered the idea that Traute Lafrenz already had one in her hands when she passed the Scholls on her way out. Yes, she herself had picked one up and kept it. While waiting for Gisela, she and Hans wandered, passing time on the third floor. Sophie admitted she impulsively pushed a stack of leaflets over the balustrade.

Fatigue from lack of sleep or the storm of questions could lead to slips of the tongue and mental confusion. Sophie tasted the coffee offered her. She did not falter, dodging incriminating responses.

Another door opened and shut tight, behind it another interrogation—Hans Fritz Scholl born on September 22, 1918. Again a personal statement could not explain the presence of the student-soldier in this prison at this time. There followed a review of school days, siblings, parents, Hitler Youth days, Reich Labor Service, military service, and furloughs for medical studies.

Interrogation records cannot show but only intimate the tenor, tone, and body language that passed between a suspect and an examiner intent upon entrapment. After the war, bookseller Josef Söhngen remembered his own experience of an intense examination that probed for information while he battled the fear of saying something that could incriminate either him or some other.

The chase began. When Hans said he went to the university to meet his girlfriend Gisela, they wanted to know if she held the same beliefs as he. He answered that she favored National Socialism, and they did not talk politics. The investigator claimed Gisela had reported otherwise.

Refusing to respond to some questions, avoiding and evading answers to others, Hans did, however, identify Alex Schmorell as a close friend and Willi Graf as an occasional visitor. Like Sophie he fielded questions about typewriters, stamps, and mail. He tried to dodge questions about the empty bags, but eventually said Sophie would fill it with sundries at home in Ulm and bring them back to Munich. The empty briefcase would protect the pipes he planned to shop for that day.

Smoke from an inquisitor's cigarette may have swirled about the room, making the atmosphere thick and heavy. A few deep drags and another round could begin.

Hans said he handwrote letters to his brother and did not use the typewriter for that purpose.

But Sophie claimed the contrary. The interrogator pit sister against brother. Investigators shared notes of the tandem proceedings, searching for inconsistencies and conflicting testimony.

Hans fired back suggesting he'd believe this only if he heard it from Sophie herself. The smoke may have cleared, but the air reeked of tension. Hans gave his version of the morning's events, admitting he called out to Gisela with a message for Alex.

A persistent question punctuated the investigation:

Wouldn't you like to tell the truth now? When the Gestapo presented Hans with condemning evidence found in the Scholls' rooms on Franz-Josef-Strasse, denial no longer served a purpose; he admitted to the production of the two recent leaflets and once more registered his protest of Hitler's continuing war with its atrocities in occupied territories. Hans attempted to implicate himself only, steering suspicion away from others. From Thursday night through Friday and into Saturday, the relentless interrogations continued. The Gestapo bombarded Hans with questions. Pressed further, he admitted to making some untrue statements, and then providing alternate explanations that suggested more active participation by others. He identified Christoph as the author of the paper he tried to destroy and hoped to reduce the impact of this information by saying Christoph did not have any intention to use it as a seventh handbill for distribution.

Time and again, Hans was exhorted to tell the whole truth. Exhorting wears many faces: pleading, prompting, goading, and inducing. The degree of intimidation or terror marking Gestapo police methods in the White Rose investigation remains concealed within the walls of Wittelsbach Palace.

On Saturday, two days after his apprehension, Hans conceded that he knew the serious nature of the Leaflets of the Resistance and accepted the operation's outcomes.

The police investigator insisted he spill more about Sophie, Alex, Willi, and Gisela. Hans pictured his sister and friends as feeding him what he needed without knowing the true use of these items: the stamps, the paper, and the envelopes. Alex, he later acknowledged, knew about the leaflets, helping to mail and carry letters, but still not aware of their contents.

More names appeared—Carl Muth and Kurt Huber.

Hans declared them academic mentors only, not cognizant of his dissident activities and citing as proof, sample scientific and philosophical topics they discussed.

The inquest turned to green paint, black tar paint, and graffiti that damned Hitler.

Hans held firm: Sophie knew nothing. But he allowed

that Alex Schmorell joined him—the men relying on night's darkness and an awareness of moonrise to shield the enterprise.

Questioning angled towards the White Rose leaflets of the past summer. When told the crime lab's findings, that both the White Rose leaflet series and the recent Leaflets of the Resistance proved the product of the same typewriter, Hans' evasions and denials ceased.

There were more exhortations.

That day, Hans again declared his credo: An alarm must awaken an intelligentsia that failed as a counterforce to the Reich's propaganda. The young man claimed he had done what others had not.

An investigator may, at any moment, engage a forceful weapon—repetition. Queries restated over and over could trigger conflicting responses, could weaken endurance, and cause a suspect to forget how he answered earlier.

A rain of White Rose questions fell on Hans: how many, to whom, with whom, how financed?

A final admonishment wrenched a final confession: Hans and Alex collaborated in the authorship, production, and distribution of the summer handbills. By Sunday, February 21, Hans' long hours of inquiry ended with his formal arrest.

Sophie had worried if her brother received brutal treatment. Tiredness had overtaken her; quiet and exhausted, she walked back to her cell. Else said she had prayed for her all night. Sophie confided: Maybe a confession will satisfy the Gestapo and no others will be implicated or subject to harm.

Mohr had lectured Sophie, praising the accomplishments of National Socialism. He tried to persuade her: Involvement with the leaflet operation was an error of judgment. Continuing, he suggested: An admission of poor judgment might soften the sentence for a conviction of high treason.

Sophie confronted Mohr saying he was the one with the distorted outlook, not she.

When Mohr leaked some of the information Hans had given over, Sophie inched toward a confession, keeping the operation of the two Leaflets of the Resistance tightly wrapped around her and her brother. Taking the opportunity, she declared their purpose as an effort to rescue the troops and the nation from a war surely to end in defeat.

For Mohr, she recollected the birth of their idea, and Alex's role as an adjunct confidante, marginally involved in preparing and mailing envelopes. She reviewed the process of the operations and related trips to multiple cities where scattered mailings would give the impression the campaign was more widespread than the work of just two people. Throughout the snarl of questions, the young suspect made plain her commitment to a central purpose: Shake up the sleeping masses and get rid of a corrupt regime.

Mohr dug for accomplices.

Sophie refused to admit recruitment.

He asked about Eickemeyer, Geyer, and her landlady.

She responded that all knew nothing.

Even under duress the deeper questions surfaced. She testified that Willi Graf knew nothing, and then continued, noting their debates about the compatibility of Christian and National Socialist beliefs and their questions surrounding "Thou shalt not kill." Sophie and Willi were fellow pilgrims; their conversations part of the journey. She told Mohr that Willi could have surmised, but she never told him about the secret operations.

Skirting Mohr's scrutiny, Sophie edged through the graffiti, treasury records, and abandoned directories. Her friends' and loves' names paraded before her.

She admitted Alex and Fritz both gave her money which she used for her own purposes.

She claimed Christoph Probst was a social friend. She knew nothing of a new draft credited to him.

She defended the innocence of Carl Muth, Otl , and Lisa.

Of the White Rose leaflets of the summer of 1942, Sophie denied having knowledge.

In the end, Mohr adjured her to see the harm her actions caused the nation and its warriors.

In the end, Sophie declared her dedication to her nation and accepted the repercussions of her behavior without regret. She believed what she did was right.

When news of another arrest filtered to Sophie's cell that weekend, she suspected Alex's capture. Later her cellmate, who also worked the registration of incoming prisoners, told her the detainee's name: Christoph Probst. Sophie's confidence and calm collapsed. Her thoughts flew to the fate of her friend's little children. She hoped the trial might be delayed long weeks, long enough so that a Nazi defeat would prevent prison sentences and executions. Then Christoph could return to his family. Sophie could not bear the terror unfolding before the young Probst family. Else listened, offering what little optimism she could muster.

Just before his arrest, Christoph was full of hope that he would be granted a leave to visit Herta in the hospital. He had arrived at the cashier anticipating a quick retrieval of his paycheck, but instead he encountered the Gestapo officers waiting for him. They wasted no time putting Christoph in manacles. He could not alert Herta to the dangers he now faced. Led to another cell in the prison, Christoph would not remain alone for long before the Gestapo's interrogations began.

A tag, strung from the lapel of his sport jacket, labeled Christoph. He had been stripped of his military uniform when the authorities apprehended him. Given civilian clothes and once out of a Luftwaffe uniform, the military no longer could protect him. Now he was held accountable only to the People's Court of the Third Reich. Light shone on the young man's face, illuminating one side and casting the other in a shadow. He squared his shoulders, and his right hand grasped his left as if to support the weight of his rigid torso. His eyes stared stone-cold into the lens of the Gestapo's camera. Christoph's usual broad, warm smile had disappeared; his lips tightened and his jaw locked. He no longer looked like Herta's husband and the father of his sons and one-month-old daughter.

In a letter written from prison, Christoph first tried to reassure his sister Angelika that he was all right even though in custody. Separation from his wife, his little ones, and his sister was hard but even more difficult was the weight his absence would place on them. He knew his children needed him. He spoke to Angelika of love, hope, and trust, closing with "Your Christel."

There were no delays as Sophie had hoped. Each received a bill of indictment: Christoph accused of composing the first draft of a leaflet; Hans charged with preparing and distributing the leaflets and for painting slogans and canceling swastikas on public buildings. The bill for Sophie cited her participation in preparing and disseminating seditious handbills. By Sunday night, February 21, 1943, the next day's court session loomed before them.

The regime flew Judge Roland Freisler from Berlin to Munich. Known for his ferocity, his presence would dramatize the importance the authorities attributed to this case. The People's Court was an unconstitutional body orchestrated by the Reich for the swift prosecution of Germans charged with crimes against the state. Hitler instituted this illegal court as a way of getting rid of opponents. It existed for the sake of processing charges of treason and other high crimes as the regime defined them. The court convened as the highest, though unlawful, tribunal of the land.

When Sophie returned to her cell, clutching the bill of indictment in her trembling hand, Else saw her ashen, drained face. She listened as Sophie moved from regret to resignation. Contemplating her own death, she thought of other young lives lost on the battlefields. Again, Sophie had refused any special consideration because she was a woman. She insisted that she and her brother shared equal responsibility. She instructed her court-appointed lawyer that if any forbearance was to be granted, it should be to Hans. He was a war veteran and should be spared the guillotine. If death should come to him, let it be by firing squad.

Realizing that tomorrow's court appearance would be a mere formality and reconciling herself to an impending death sentence, Sophie's consolation was the thought that a student revolt would surely happen soon.

Robert Mohr advised Sophie to write her final letters before the next day's court session. Many letters had circulated through the family in all the years of her growing up—letters that spoke of home and Mother's kindnesses and Father's firm guidance. Letters to Lisa had planned mountain excursions, and letters to Otl had honed her mind in the pondering or debating of some philosophical question. Letters whispering of longing and love had traveled over battlefields to Fritz. Now these letters would be the last.

The winter sun set, and as Sophie lay on her cot, thoughts lingered around her brothers and sisters and parents. Else listened closely to Sophie's concerns for the loss her loved ones would feel. Soon there was silence, and Else watched as Sophie slipped into a deep sleep.

Sophie sank into a dream. In her arms she held a baby in a christening gown. She felt herself climbing a hill, moving forward until she came to a cavernous break in the road, somewhat like the fissure in a glacier. Sophie reached out over the abyss and placed the baby safely on the other side. Then she tumbled into darkness. When Sophie awoke, she told her dream, saying the child represented their idea that would survive even though she would not.

It was not long before Else reached her hand out to Sophie for a final farewell. When Sophie walked out of her prison cell, she left behind the bill of indictment. On its blank side she left a final message in bold letters: *Freiheit*, freedom.

Hans, too, left his imprint in Wittelsbach, scribbling on the cell's white wall advice his father had often borrowed from Goethe—a command: Hold firm and hold your own under pressure.

Outside Wittelsbach, two cars waited. Two officers escorted Sophie to one vehicle. Christoph and Hans, having endured their final night in prison, were led to a second car.

# Chapter Sixteen

# A HIGHER COURT

MAGDALENE SCHOLL BAKED COOKIES. It did not matter that her children were young adults; she looked forward to their visits to Ulm and prepared the sweets for them and their friends as she always had. Traute traveled to the Cathedral Square apartment for the weekend as had been planned earlier. She confirmed the news that would change Magdalene's life forever. The young medical student shared what she knew of Hans' and Sophie's arrest in Munich. By chance, Werner was home on leave.

Late that weekend, when Jürgen Wittenstein picked up the phone to call the Scholls, he knew the conversation could very well be wiretapped. Discovery worried him as it others with even the slightest connection to the White Rose. The message: Tomorrow, at ten in the morning, Sophie and Hans would appear in court. The Scholls should leave Ulm as soon as possible. Jürgen promised to meet them at the railway station and take them to the Palace of Justice.

Showing up in a public place and even being seen with Herr and Frau Scholl could place Jürgen in jeopardy, but that Monday when the Ulm train slid into the terminal, he hurried the distraught parents away. The trial had already begun.

On February 22, 1943, a crowd of invited spectators swept toward the Palace of Justice. Outdoors, archways framed a courtyard surrounded by a building rising dramatically to a second and third level. Balconies hung beneath huge deep windows. Indoors, the Court of Assizes Chamber readied for the trial of three Munich students. The massive wooden dais stretched along a wall where a spindled railing corralled the official proceedings. The room hushed as the three defendants, two refined, handsome-looking young men and a wholesome German girl, entered the court chambers. Their apparent self-possession and dignified manner, despite their dire predicament, amazed some on-lookers. With quiet solemnity they took their places before the justices.

Today's trial was one of a very few resistance cases brought to public attention. Knowledge of the White Rose incident had spread throughout the community. The consequences of their actions, according to the regime, had to be circulated among the Volk, especially among the students.

Freisler's rhetoric fired up the proceedings.

The indictment drawn up by the Reich's attorney was read, charging Sophie, Hans, and Christoph with high treason. The youths were considered enemies of the state who had endangered the nation with the production and distribution of seditious leaflets. The indictment described the three as aiding and abetting the enemy and weakening the resolve of the Wehrmacht as well as the will of the people to stay the course of the war. The document declared that the students' conspiratorial actions took place in numerous cities: Munich, Augsburg, Salzburg, Vienna, Stuttgart, and Linz with the intention of advancing regime change and recruiting others to organize for these purposes.

Hysteria emanated from the red-robed Judge Freisler whose rigid movements and taut face nearly exploded as he broke loose in a frenzied attack against the three youths.

A courtroom window reached nearly from floor to ceiling. Set deep into the walls, light poured through at given moments, illuminating the dark proceedings.

Jürgen and the Scholls rushed to the Palace of Justice

where the trial had already begun. Because safety kept Jürgen from going farther, Frau and Herr Scholl and Werner had to work their way into the courtroom where invited big-wigs and party supporters filled the benches. By some contrivance, Robert, Magdalene, and Werner gained entry.

Spectators sat riveted to their places as attention focused on the youths and their ideas being prosecuted that late morning. The students' words, the Professor's thoughts, and Christoph's draft echoed throughout the room as each leaflet was read aloud.

Insulting, berating, and attempting to demonize and dishonor the defendants, Freisler's spectacle raged on. He accused: The defendants stole supplies for their treasonous acts. With courage and conviction Sophie shouted that their words represented the silent voice of many people. She had chosen to make that voice heard.

As the trial neared completion, Werner watched his brother, sister, and Christoph under the scrutinizing eyes of the Director of the Regional (Bavarian) Judiciary Steir, as well as SS Group Leader Breithaupt, SA Group Leader Bunge, State Secretary and SA Group Leader Köglmaier, and Reich Attorney Weyersberg. Frau Scholl agonized as her children, though calm and upright, suffered a barrage of attacks. Her own strength drained from her as she crumbled in near collapse. A temporary recess from the room helped her to regain her composure.

Robert Scholl could hardly contain his frustration with the court-appointed attorney whose lack of argument belied a lack of interest in defense. Words burst from Herr Scholl as he raised his voice in behalf of the three young defendants. Freisler, the hanging judge, banished the family from the courtroom, but not before Robert cried out, invoking the higher court that would ultimately judge all.

Finally, in early afternoon, the judge called a recess for deliberation. The halls swelled with courtroom observers. Just a short time elapsed before they all filled the chamber once again. The doors closed, and Robert, Magdalene, and Werner remained alone, barred from witnessing the inevitable sentencing.

There was no delay in the announcement.

The People's Court found Christoph Hermann Probst, Sophia Magdalena Scholl, and Hans Fritz Scholl guilty of high treason, undermining National Socialism, insulting Hitler, and helping the Reich's enemies.

The punishment: Death by guillotine.

The court insisted on keeping the appearance of a legal authority using an established due process. It called each defendant for last words.

Earlier Sophie had spoken; she now remained silent.

Christoph, for the sake of Herta, Michael, Vincent, and his infant daughter, begged for clemency. He explained that the German losses at the Battle of Stalingrad threw him into a state of psychotic depression, so much so, that it affected his state of mind when he wrote the note that condemned him. Further, he defended: The added anxiety of his wife Herta's hospitalization had created extraordinary stress.

Hans had no last words for himself. Instead, he implored the court to heed Christoph's plea.

Freisler abruptly cut him off, silencing him.

In the hallway a young lawyer, Leo Samberger, sought out the Scholl family. He moved forward, greeting them with sympathetic words expressing his disgust with the court's behavior. He had observed the three youths and admired the conviction they demonstrated, even under the extreme pressure of the authorities' attempts to discredit them. His advice got the Scholls' full attention: Approach the National Prosecutor with an appeal for clemency. Samberger said he would help.

Magdalene and Robert did not waste a moment and set out to initiate an appeal.

The mother and father searched for the right words trying to sway the court's severe punishment. They held out alternatives like prison terms, or for Hans, assignment to serve on the Eastern front. They called upon their children's past achievements as good students, and Hans' record as a good soldier working under the guidance of well-respected doctors in the field hospitals. Robert and Magdalene described their son and daughter as inexperienced idealists troubled by recent stresses. Sophia's fiancé served in Stalingrad and had been hospitalized, the family's finances were unstable, and their brother Werner served on the Eastern front. They asked for clemency for their son and daughter. Werner registered a plea on behalf of his brother and sister, hoping his own status in the military would have some influence. Almost as a postscript, Magdalene and Robert asked for permission to speak with Hans and Sophie.

At approximately two in the afternoon, five hours after the trial ordeal had begun, the authorities transported Hans, Sophie, and Christoph from the Palace of Justice to the prison at Stadelheim in a suburb of Munich. Next door—the Perlach Forest and the cemetery.

The prison warden and guards at Stadelheim witnessed scores of inmates enduring last hours on death row. Monday afternoon, handcuffed Sophie Scholl marched to one of the cells. On the wall hung a crucifix; a window filtered light as afternoon turned to evening. The guards monitored the calm and quiet twenty-one-year-old student dressed in an outfit that looked like she was heading off to shop or to school.

Visits to prisoners awaiting execution at Stadelheim were generally forbidden, but Magdalene and Robert's request to speak with their children had been granted. Werner joined them for the meeting.

First Hans, already garbed in a prison uniform, entered the room. He looked at his parents, and they looked at him. Magdalene offered a bit of candy; Hans refused. He reassured them that he held no animosity toward anyone. Robert wrapped his arms around Hans, promising that history would remember him. Hans felt the strength of his father's embrace. A few last messages and a tear escaped. Magdalene and Robert watched him disappear.

Then Sophie came into the room. Again Magdalene offered candy, and Sophie accepted saying she hadn't had any lunch. Understanding her parents' pain, she sought to console her mother who lamented that she would never come home again.

Sophie gently soothed her mother. A few fleeting

moments, a few more sentiments exchanged, and Sophie walked away from her parents. The Scholls left the prison, still thinking that the plea Samberger sought might change the sentence.

Soft tears escaped after Sophie's last farewell to her parents. The flavor of Mother's candy dissolved. She held in her heart Magdalene's words reminding her of Jesus.

Robert, Magdalene, and Werner left, hoping for a pardon. A Protestant chaplain visited with Hans and Sophie to pray the psalms.

A Catholic priest hastened to Christoph and prepared the water and oil for his baptism. Christoph had long ago denounced evil; he had always been a believer. The sacrament confirmed his deepest faith in an All-Mighty beyond the reaches of the Führer. The chaplain offered a consecrated wafer, and Christoph received communion. He would leave his wife and children, but he had faith their relationship would continue forever. He prepared himself for the waiting he would do until the day of their eternal reunion. In that final hour, though alone and without the comfort of his family, Christoph wrote to his mother, thanking her for his life and promising to wait for her in the world to come.

Herta did not know that this hour was her husband's last.

AT FIVE O'CLOCK THE PRISON GUARDS allowed Sophie, Hans, and Christoph a moment together. Puffs of smoke enveloped them as they passed a cigarette, each inhaling and exhaling in a final act of solidarity. Christoph broke into the silence, assuring his friends they would meet shortly in eternity.

The guards took Sophie first. Calmly and with dignity she walked to the guillotine.

Then they took Hans. Hans who had hoped to survive and to serve a new Germany after the war, now resigned himself to his fate. His very last word sounded from the executioner's block—freedom.

Then they took Christoph.

The night's shadow covered Munich. The Scholl family

still harbored a thread of hope. But there was no clemency, and as they soon learned, there was no time. Hans and Sophie were buried outside Stadelheim near Perlach Forest.

Within a few days, Christoph's brother Dieter received a telegram from Angelika Probst. She urged him to come home quickly, saying their mother was ill. Dieter managed to get a short leave. That night he entered a church sanctuary in the French village where he was stationed. He picked up a prayer book and opened to a random page, and read the verse, "He is not dead; he has passed into another life." When Dieter arrived in Munich and learned the truth, he remembered the passage.

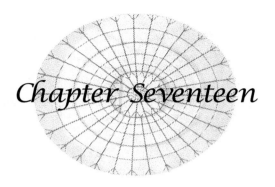

# Chapter Seventeen

# CONVICTIONS

SKIES DARKENED AS AN APPROACHING STORM loomed over the mountains where a solitary figure sought refuge under the forest's canopy. Alex was on the run again after someone recognized him in the town where a Russian acquaintance had offered shelter. His clothes would barely protect him from the elements of an ordinary winter day; even the blanket given him by the Russian coachman was little help. Now his body worked desperately to keep warm. Alex had little choice: forge ahead toward Switzerland or retreat to the city where authorities patrolled the streets searching for him. He chose the mountains. An avid, experienced mountaineer, Alex braced for the winter snowstorm and the windblown snow that steals vision and makes feet grow heavy. When conditions worsened, he reconsidered, having only himself to consult and advise. He turned his back on Switzerland.

Days had passed since Alex stood in the crowd gathered outside the university. Six days since he had last seen Hans and Sophie, it was not yet a week that the Gestapo whisked them away. Since his flight from Munich, newspapers continued to carry notices of his physical description, offering generous rewards for his capture.

Alex knew he would have to conceal his identity as he slipped back into Munich's Schwabing neighborhood, but fate would not give him time. The sudden, shrill whine of an air raid alert threw the streets into high anxiety as citizens scrambled for cover. Mothers grabbed their children and students ran to the nearest shelters. All of them packed into underground bunkers—all lined the crowded basements with anticipation and dread as the roar of Allied bombers bore down on them. Alex rushed for safety with the rest. In the confusion, he recognized the familiar face of an old girlfriend among the strangers in the bunker. Maybe she could help him. The young woman saw Alex but so did the others surrounding her; they remembered the picture of the young man hunted by the authorities. When the all clear sounded and the crowds poured into the city streets once more, Marie Luise denounced Alex.

A vehicle's doors swung open, and Gestapo officers jumped out to sweep another member of the White Rose from the streets of Munich. As the guards ushered Alex into prison, he prepared to take all the blame. Interrogations would soon begin. He did not know that Hans, Sophie, and Christoph already lay buried in Perlach Cemetery.

Three days later, on February 27th, a house in Gräfelfing lay silent. It was early morning, not quite dawn when Birgit's warning cry pierced her father's sleep. Jolted into wakefulness, Kurt Huber opened his eyes to confront three dark figures towering over him. Twelve-year-old Birgit had no one to help her; Mother and brother Wolfi had gone to the country. Questioning, searching, the Gestapo completed their mission. Birgit watched in horror as the men stole her father from her. Again the house was silent.

Imprisonment could not stop Kurt from his teaching. Each day he picked up his pen and began to write and shape and mold, line by line, paragraph by paragraph, a work he hoped would be his legacy. There may have been days when a battered and bruised Huber, as some reports suggest, quietly swallowed the pains inflicted from maltreatment. He lost himself in thought deep and sublime as he chronicled the life story of Leibniz, a philosopher of great standing in the classical world, but a character with no redeeming qualities in the Nazi worldview. Precious moments passed into hours as the once respected teacher scratched on leaves of paper a work he hoped would raise the thoughts of future students who might read it.

A letter from Clara and news of home fed Kurt's spirits. He worried about the hunger his family must be experiencing, for he, too, was hungry for their companionship. He did not know that Clara's letters were a lie and that she was in prison, held in kinship arrest and forced to write the untrue messages. He did not know the authorities ordered Birgit to tell anyone who might ask for her parents that they were away on a vacation.

The Reich insisted: The family of a traitor must be held accountable. As the weeks of the February executions, arrests, and imprisonments stretched into spring, other families of White Rose members were rounded up. Magdalene Scholl, her health failing daily, had already served time in solitary since the execution of her children two months earlier. On a Sunday evening, Robert, also held in custody, would write a long letter to his surviving family. But even Father's loving thoughts could not stop the diphtheria-like illness that afflicted Inge during her imprisonment. Elisabeth's kidney ailment set her free from *Sippenhaft,* leaving her to roam the streets friendless except for the loyal support of Fritz Hartnagel. Occasionally, there was a letter from Werner who had been spared prison but sent back to the Eastern front. He would never return.

Days grew long and lonely in early April when contacts with Ulm, and voices from outside the Reich, were no longer within range. If family members held in clan arrest could have heard a Voice of America broadcast, Paul Tillich's message may have heartened them, for news of what had happened in Munich seeped into the free world. Tillich, an eminent Protestant theologian and professor, had been banned from German universities years earlier by the Nazis wishing to silence his opposition. Unable to teach any longer in Germany, he found sanctuary at the Union Theological Seminary in New York City. In 1943, Germans who listened secretly to his broadcasts heard his messages chronicling growing resistance. A tally of

bravery followed his usual salutation, "My Fellow Germans."
Tillich reported: Belgian bishops protest slave labor; Norwe-
gians destroy munitions factories; underground presses
expand. Then he announced that German students had been
killed because of their pamphlets heralding the downfall of all
that was good in Germany. Word of the White Rose was
spreading beyond the Fatherland. Tillich ended his address
urging German citizens to free themselves from the Reich's
tyranny. To extricate themselves now would liberate the spirit
when the tyrannical regime had been destroyed once and for
all.

Snatches of news of others connected to the White Rose
reached those in prison. It was on Good Friday, April 23, 1943,
when Inge heard what had happened during the previous days
of Holy Week, the same week when Tillich's address from
America traced a history of Good Fridays during the Nazi
reign, speaking of the suffering in camps, prisons, and battlefields, mourning the tragedy overtaking the world.

On the Monday of Holy Week, April 19, 1943, in the city
of Warsaw, Germans had plans to finish off what little remained
in the ghetto. Just nine months earlier members of the Second
Student Company had passed through the city on their way to
the Russian front, leaving its deep impression on Willi. Now it
was also Passover, the Jewish festival of freedom, and on that
day the last remaining men and women, after thousands of others had been deported, staged a surprise revolt against their
tormentors, killing some German soldiers and for awhile ward-
ing off their oppressors. In the midst of the chaos and destruction, a freedom fighter remembers seeing a family sitting
around the holiday table, their Passover ritual accompanied by
the explosive screams in the streets.

INGE HEARD FRAGMENTS of what had transpired that Holy Week.
Fourteen individuals associated with the White Rose knew
more.

Early Monday morning, on April 19th, a van had halted
near an entrance to the Palace of Justice. The authorities pulled
together a collection of university students, a few high school

students, and a couple adults, now delivering fourteen individuals to the People's Court for the second round of White Rose trials. They had good reason to be apprehensive. It was no secret what had happened to Sophie, Christoph, and Hans in these chambers.

Many, like Professor Kurt Huber, Alex Schmorell and Willi Graf had been subjected to relentless investigation since their February arrests. Others had been rounded up in the weeks since then. Now judgment would come to each at the bench of the hot-blooded Roland Freisler who had returned from Berlin ready for another bout with the Munich dissidents. Garbed in his flaming red gown, he marched into the room ready to do battle. Four other judges shadowed him. Again the chambers crowded with ranking civil and military personages committed to total war since Stalingrad.

A solemn recitation of the defendants' names and charges brought against each of them opened the proceedings that were to last a grueling fourteen hours. As during the first White Rose trials, a public reading of the leaflets commenced.

An officious voice called Alexander Schmorell before the tribunal. Having heard the charges of high treason held against him, Alex braved a defense, claiming as he had during interrogations that as the son of a Russian mother he preferred to build bridges of understanding between the German and Russian people. He confessed that serious mental reservations about National Socialism had caused him great emotional anxiety.

Freisler's temper percolated: This objection was nonsense, pure foolishness.

Alex persisted, admitting that, while serving on the Eastern front, he had resolved never to take aim and shoot a Russian. Near a rolling boil, the judge charged him to explain exactly what he did, then, on the Russian plains.

Alex reminded the judge that he did what a medic in the fields was expected to do, tend to the sick and offer aid to the wounded. He confessed that his convictions were not conveniently formulated for the sake of a defense, but that at his induction into the Wehrmacht he had, because of conscientious objection, tried to avoid pledging allegiance to Hitler. Alex's forthrightness triggered an explosion.

Freisler's fury silenced the young defendant and banished him from the stand.

The People's Court refused to consider what it deemed individual eccentricities. Adolf Hitler commanded obedience and service to the common cause. This Monday, April 19, 1943, was the eve of Adolf Hitler's birthday, for years a national day of celebration throughout Germany. The past ten years echoed the sounds of huge assemblies of children and throngs of citizens lining the streets as Hitler's motorcade passed by. It was a time when parents handed over their ten-year-old sons to the Hitler Youth, and they in turn gave the Führer a birthday gift, their solemn oath of allegiance. They promised to obey when they listened to his impassioned words: "Nothing is possible unless one will commands and the others always obey, starting at the top and ending at the very bottom."

On the eve of Hitler's birthday, Alex ill-timed his plea for recognition of personal values.

The name Wilhelm Graf next filled the chamber. Willi's quiet, measured demeanor brought a temporary calm after the last volcanic examination. Willi listened as the court recounted all they had learned about his journey through the Rhineland, encouraging old friends to join in the resistance. His careful, calculated conduct during his imprisonment had led his interrogators to dark alleys and dead ends in their attempts to wrench names of collaborators from him. Now that Freisler had Willi pinned in front of the tribunal, the judge glowered: You may think that your evasion sabotaged the Gestapo, but we have proven ourselves far smarter than you. When Willi turned silent, his back towards his examiner, he knew he had remained as loyal as he could to his friends and others on trial today. The Courtroom watched, waiting for the inflammatory Roland Freisler to fan his indignation, his boisterous outbursts fueling a conflagration of insult and rage against the remaining defendants.

Called forth after the two youths, fifty-one-year-old Kurt Huber stepped forward, clutching the notes he had prepared as another challenge to the court. He no longer bore the title Professor or Doctor; he had been stripped of his status and pension, leaving his family destitute. But, as he was later to tell the court, they could not take away the integrity of his inner being. Now he would speak for himself with the same conviction he so frequently demonstrated in the lecture hall when his words slowly erased all notice of his infirmities. He faced his opponents like the true German patriot he considered himself.

He admitted there was not a word to repudiate. But there was an explanation.

Referring to his draft entitled "Statement of the Accused," Huber approached the heart of the matter—the role and responsibilities of a teacher. It was his duty, he reasoned, to guide students in their examination of ideas, events, and behaviors, both their own and those of the state. He argued that it was not against the law to encourage students to observe the dichotomy between the state's actions and an ideal social contract.

Freisler's antagonism and hostility punctuated Huber's statement.

Huber stood firm, plying his way through reason and uttering words like: trust, security, and self-determination.

Freisler shot a command to cease the lecture.

Huber clawed his way through to the finish maintaining the rightness of his criticism and calling for freedom for Germans.

Before he limped back to his place, the Professor petitioned the court to consider his family.

There was no compassion.

Despite his arguments, the tribunal asserted that this man had abused his position as teacher when he advanced what they called visions of a federal, multi-party democratic system for Germany's future. He bated his students, they claimed, with thoughts of an individualism that ran counter to the very obedience necessary to energize the National Socialistic values promoted by the Führer.

The morning turned to afternoon and dragged into evening. One after another the threads of the White Rose network unraveled as each defendant stood before the judges. Franz Müller, Susanne Hirzel, Heinrich Guter, Gisela Schertling, Katharina Schüddekopf, and Traute Lafrenz. Hungry and thirsty, they readied themselves for the tribunal's return and the verdicts.

After deliberation, Freisler and his cohorts delivered their decisions.

Among those waiting were two of Willi's friends from the *Neudeutschland*. One was Heinrich Bollinger, just a few days away from his 27th birthday. The other, Helmut Bauer, a twenty-three year old from Saarbrücken, had been charged with not reporting what he knew about the White Rose. They had, the court asserted, endangered the German nation by listening. First, they listened to Willi Graf's news about the Munich group—perhaps under cover of darkness—perhaps on the platform of the railway station as Willi prepared to leave on his recruitment tour of the Rhineland. But they *had* listened and not reported. Then too, they listened to forbidden foreign radio broadcasts. The two young men defended themselves saying they listened to hear news about Munich.

The Court retorted: Why would good Germans listen to foreign correspondence for such news? Nonsense! Now as the People's Court delivered the verdicts and imposed sentences, the entreaties of the two proved fruitless. The decree—Seven years each.

An account also had to be settled with Eugene Grimminger who handed over 500 marks to Hans and Alex in Stuttgart more than once. The decree—Ten years.

The transcripts of the sentences imposed that Monday, April 19, recite a litany of teenagers and young adults cast into prison for months or years.

Teenager Hans Hirzel's forays into pamphlet posting with Sophie cost him five years. A misguided youth, the Court proclaimed, led astray by his associations with the evil Scholls.

Franz Josef Müller was sentenced to five years for falling under the influence of others intending to undermine the Reich and for addressing and preparing leaflets for distribution.

Heinrich Guter, another Ulm teenager, was punished

with eighteen months for not reporting what he knew about propaganda urging resistance.

Traute Lafrenz, so close to the inner circle, was not perceived as a serious threat by the court. They thought her a foolish girl, ready to admit her wrongs after failing to report what she knew to the authorities. They knew she had been at the summer farewell party before the medical students were sent to Russia. They underestimated her involvement—One year.

Katharina Schüddekopf was seen as a girl who, though she attended the gatherings at Eickemeyer's studio, was essentially on the fringes but still to be held accountable for not reporting seditious talk. Punishment—One year.

Susan Hirzel was viewed as an innocent girl who had made the mistake of not asking what was in the envelopes her brother asked her to post. For this—six months.

Gisela Schertling, Hans' most recent girlfriend and friend of Sophie, was recognized not as a willful participant but brought into the situation by circumstance. The court admonished that despite evidence that her greater interest was in Hans Scholl and not dissidence, she should have reported what she had discovered about the operation. Her punishment—One year.

Falk Harnack, Hans and Alex's hope for connection to a wider resistance, was set free. The explanation—A special situation. He must have failed to report the visits from Hans and Alex because of the stress of his brother's and sister-in-law's executions. Besides, his original plays were popular among the soldiers at the front. Perhaps the investigators believed they could trail him and be led to other resisters.

Kurt Huber, the tribunal contended, had hammered a wedge between the Army and the regime. He had planted doubt in the minds of his students. That was enough, along with his participation in the leaflet campaign, to condemn him to death.

Alex Schmorell, they said, had pledged his allegiance to Hitler despite his hyphenated identity, his Russian mother. He was a German sworn to Germany and charged with high treason—punishable by death.

They knew of Willi's recruiting missions, his graffiti escapades, his visits to Eickemeyer's studio and the philosophical debates. They knew all they needed in order to send Willi Graf to his death.

A van opened its doors outside the Palace of Justice. Guards herded the men and women into the vehicle and slammed the door. Locked inside were resignation, separation's grim reality, and hope. Maybe the war's end would set them free.

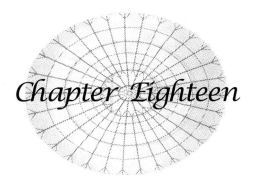

# Chapter Eighteen

# TO LIFE

A N ANXIOUS SIEGFRIED DIESINGER approached the young man
on death row. Alex was a promise unfulfilled—his medicine, his music, his art—the potential that would never materialize. Siegfried had not abandoned him but occasionally joined
the prisoner for quiet conversation. The lawyer greeted Alex,
and in return Alex welcomed the defense counselor whose
arguments had failed during the April trial. The fault lay with
a People's Court that gave mere lip service to due process. They
still awaited a response to the appeal for clemency circulating
through the military ranks. It would finally reach Hitler.
Siegfried detected no panic or regret as he listened to Alex's
assurance that the work had been right, the effort correct.
Diesinger marveled at the young man's calm even as death
drew closer.

The petition for clemency returned; Hitler rejected any
commutation of the death sentence.

BEYOND THE PRISON WALLS, the Führer accelerated the elimination
of Jews, calling the plan, the Final Solution. By mid-June 1943,
the Nazis resolved to empty the ghettos of Poland and the
Soviet Union and fill the death camps.

The disaster at Stalingrad heralded a renewed attempt to restore the Wehrmacht's prestige. The Führer's desire, to once and for all crush Russia, fueled an aggressive mood at the beginning of the summer of 1943. The Wehrmacht's past triumphs had taken place during this season, so the promise of another victory seemed credible. Hitler primed himself and the German armored divisions for Operation *Zitadelle*, proclaiming, "The victory of Kursk must be as a beacon to the whole world."

New German tanks rumbled to the East; hundreds and thousands of metal hulks churned through the fields. With confidence anchored to a vast army of tanks, the Russians waited patiently as throngs of soldiers amassed for battle on the 5th of July. A fiery week exploded when the raging machinery tore across the terrain, raining fragments of flesh and metal on Germans and Russians alike. By the 12th of July, corpses littered the smoking battlefields, and Hitler, thwarted once again, was forced to withdraw.

Six months earlier, Professor Huber's leaflet had demanded an end to murderous ambitions. The words that had protested the carnage at Stalingrad now echoed in the fields of Kursk where slaughter prevailed. The morning of July 13, 1943, the day of Alex's and Professor Huber's execution, arrived in the shadow of that monstrous battle.

Kurt Huber's words had sped across the paper, charging to the next thought, racing against time; he still had two remaining chapters to finish for his Leibniz manuscript. The Reich had denied his petition for extra time to complete the work. The moment came for the writing to stop.

When dawn broke on that July morning, Huber faced his last hours. A bottle of wine, a bouquet of Alpine roses, both gifts from his wife Clara, wrapped him in loving thoughts. Kurt raised a drink to his family and to his country. His pen moved again, now in a final farewell, rallying his devotion to freedom and envisioning his death as a journey to the mountaintop. Then he bestowed a final blessing upon his loved ones.

Alex offered forgiveness, releasing any trace of anger or hatred for his denouncer. The months in prison had pulled him into deeper self-examination and meditation. Writing to his parents, he spoke of belief and God, reassuring them peace had entered his heart. His final message expressed a firm conviction that he had lived seeking the truth. His thoughts turned to young lives lost on battlefields and others, like his own, at the executioner's block. Alex promised never to forget his loved ones, ending his message, "Yours, Schurik."

Nearly five months after Hans, Sophie, and Christoph left death row, the guards escorted Alex and Professor Huber from their prison cells.

First they took Alex, the young medic, student-soldier, the artist, and the co-author of the first White Rose leaflet that had insisted on the responsibility of every individual to fight totalitarianism. Day ended; it was early evening, and night would soon descend. Alex walked across the courtyard to the guillotine.

Reverend Brinkmann watched from a prison window as Professor Huber carried himself with dignity and reached the door to the outbuilding. There was nothing more to be done. His thoughts had driven his deeds, even unto the end. Reverend Brinkmann made the sign of the cross when Kurt Huber disappeared to meet death.

EACH DAY SINCE HIS ARREST in February and the trial in April, Willi Graf waited at the edge of uncertainty. Robert Mohr had worked him hard during the interrogations, aiming to uncover more about his Catholic associates. Willi met Mohr's question with vague answers, claiming he could not remember details or insisting his conversations with certain individuals remained only generally political or strictly personal in nature.

Mohr might shout out a name.

Willi would counter: The name is unfamiliar.

Even those he acknowledged like the Bollingers, Harnack, Muth, Lafrenz, he softened with disclaimers. With some he had little contact; others he placed on the fringes of situations, trying to dilute or distance their connections to the dissident effort. Mohr's impatience demanded more straightforward responses; the interrogator relied on exhortations to open up Willi's testimony.

Willi prayed for bravery and strength. He might be coaxed with promises of hard labor instead of death if he would just talk more. He could have been tempted. He might have been able to survive hard labor and maybe someday reunite with his family. From the end of February until the end of March, Willi endured at least nine sessions, all the while worrying about the consequences for his family and trying to veer any suspicion away from them. He agonized over the knowledge that his actions had fractured the family's stability. Eight days after his arrest in February, the authorities had wrenched Herr and Frau Graf from their home and locked them in prison for two months. The explanation was simple: Your son is accused of high treason.

Anneliese, after her separation from Willi upon their detention, found herself in a cell with Angelika Probst, Christoph's sister. She had listened to the young woman speak of her brother and talked of her own. When she heard of Christoph's execution, she tried to comfort the grieving Angelika. Yet, Willi still lived. In the cloud of sorrow that hung over the sisters' cell, Anneliese tried not to despair. For four months the women clung to each other's company. Mathilde had escaped *Sippenhaft* at the time of Willi's arrest because she was three months away from delivering her baby.

When the Reich freed Anneliese from clan arrest, she journeyed to her brother; the delay in Willi's execution gave her hope. Perhaps trying to console Willi, she suggested: Maybe the postponement means there's still a chance for a pardon. Willi had his doubts. The only clarity Anneliese perceived was in her brother's blue eyes that appeared to see beyond the present moment.

Long sheets of white paper rested before Willi. Ordered to write an autobiography, thoughts turned first to family, the family captured in photographs that lay somewhere now in the house in Saarbrücken. It had been eighteen years since Willi, Mathilde, and Anneliese had lined up for a formal portrait with big sister Mathilde on the left, a huge bow resting like a crown on her head, and little sister Anneliese in the middle, curled between her older siblings. Willi, on the right, blonde and boyish in a navy suit, an anchor insignia on the left sleeve, leaned forward in a relaxed pose. As he wrote, he remembered a childhood filled with warmth and order, when love tempered discipline and commitment in the family circle. He filled the blank sheets of paper, sketching the landscape of his life and recording reminiscences of his father and mother, taking the time to draw attention to his mother's deep affection and devotion.

The words rolled out the story of school days, music lessons, playtime and vacations, and gave way to commentary on abiding faith in spiritual matters. When Willi reached page ten and a half, he stopped the story of his life. The economy of words only hinted at the inner depth of his being.

EVEN AFTER HANS, SOPHIE, CHRISTOPH, Alex, and Professor Huber had been executed, and while Willi still languished behind bars, copies of the sixth leaflet began to reappear with an added banner proclaiming the spirit of the White Rose still lived.

Another young man at the University of Munich had reason to carry on the protest and call for resistance. He had been thrown out of the University of Hamburg because his mother was from a Jewish family, but he had been given shelter at the University of Munich under the wing of a professor who disregarded the Nazi laws prohibiting half-Jews. The youth hated the Nuremberg laws and found in the Leaflets of Resistance a voice for his protest. He and his girlfriend typed copies and distributed them, making a connection with friends in Hamburg. Later, while collecting money for Kurt Huber's wife and children, Hans Leipelt was caught, imprisoned, and executed.

Jürgen Wittenstein, too, collected money to financially aid the Hubers. His devotion and admiration for his teacher supported the risky business. Later, Jürgen volunteered for the Italian front to escape Gestapo inquiries as they became increasingly wary of his associations with sympathizers.

When the text of a leaflet reached Helmuth James von Moltke, a young German lawyer employed by the German intelligence service, he took it with him to Sweden. Helmuth worked to stem the Reich's aggressive actions, using his power of persuasion and holding firm to his strong Christian faith and his belief in non-violence. He hoped for a quick end to the war and dreamed of a democratic state. Following the call to duplicate and distribute the Munich handbill, he made sure it traveled from Sweden to England. Shortly, Germans, secretly listening to BBC broadcasts, heard the voice of the White Rose. Thousands of leaflets were reproduced and the Royal Air Force scattered them, sending them floating onto German soil.

HERR AND FRAU GRAF'S RELEASE FROM DETENTION initiated their earnest efforts to save their only son's life. Three days after the announced death penalty, Willi's father wrote an appeal to Hitler on the occasion of the Führer's birthday. Gerhard Graf hoped his reputation as a staunch Party member with a history of correct attitudes would modify the death sentence to a long prison term. After all, his pub had hosted important large Party gatherings in Saarbrücken, especially at the time of the Saarland's return to Germany.

Mathilde's husband, an experienced soldier, wrote letters on behalf of his brother-in-law, urging the courts to consider his youth and the probability of his rehabilitation within a family supporting the Reich. Willi could prove himself through a transfer to the front. Character references from Willi's comrades, evaluations of his service by Chief Medical Officers, and arguments from the Grafs' lawyer had little effect. Willi remained imprisoned despite their hopes that a delayed execution of his sentence bought time, time that might deliver amnesty.

Hitler refused to grant clemency.

Lonely and isolated, Willi asked Anneliese to send him the poetry of Friedrich Hölderlin. Willi had survived the grueling war in Russia by retreating, when he could, into the imaginative realms of poetry and literature. In Willi's cell, Hölderlin's company could transport the young man to a world where the mystical and religious mingled with ancient gods in visions of ecstatic experience. The verses could inspire or comfort with dreams of home.

As Mathilde's delivery date approached, Willi felt sure the baby was a boy. It heartened him to think that the child would arrive at a time when his departure seemed imminent.

In early May, Joachim was born. Even in his confinement, Willi felt joy, sending his welcome to the little boy. A small piece of paper was barely room enough for all the affection he longed to share with them. He rejoiced that his family could focus on a new life, and that Herr and Frau Graf, now grandparents, would find some delight in an otherwise bleak circumstance. Joachim, Willi thought, would take his place; the boy would be a consolation.

It was late September and finally Mathilde would have more than an hour with Willi. Little Joachim was nearly five months old, and Willi often pictured the infant boy surrounded by the family circle that had nurtured him as a child. Now he would hear more. Willi's sister considered the visitor's permit a precious gift, giving her the chance to listen to her brother as he unburdened thoughts that shackled him day after day. She assured him that the Gestapo had not brought more harm to the family.

He wondered: What about friends? Were they free?

Mathilde spoke of the kindness the neighbors had shown the Grafs.

Before their time together ended, Willi begged her to tell their father that his actions were serious and not frivolous. Time would show his deeds honorable.

When October arrived, the time had come to say good-bye, quietly and secretly. Chaplain Heinrich Speer shifted the scraps of paper and readied himself for the message Willi would dictate.

Willi told Anneliese that he held close the letter she had written.

The chaplain scribbled in shorthand, each line and symbol crammed onto the first slip of paper, just 7 by 10.5 cm.

Willi continued his dictation, trusting his parents to Anneliese's care and reminding her of his deep affection and admiration.

When one slip of paper filled, the chaplain moved on to the next.

Willi continued, assuring his family of his prayers and his submission to God's will. He asked Anneliese to tell them once again that his actions represented his response to the grave circumstances of the times.

The loops and dashes and dots moved onto another slip. Willi went on and the chaplain transcribed.

He gave special attention to his godson, Joachim, calling upon those remaining to give faithful support to the child.

Sentiments of love and suffering, sorrow and hope continued. He told Anneliese to think of him when she heard music, especially the aria from Handel's *Messiah*—"I know that my Redeemer liveth," a musical piece whose message proclaimed, "...but we shall all be changed, in a moment, in the twinkling of an eye, at the last trumpet."

Just a few blank scraps remained when Willi asked the chaplain to address the next message to his mother, professing his love.

Knowing the next sentence would be his last, Willi took the paper from the chaplain and added in his own handwriting a message of strength and courage, finally signing, "Your Willi."

On October 12, 1943, Willi walked across the yard to the outbuilding where the executioner awaited. Swiftly, in the count of eleven seconds, it was over.

That October, Gerhard Graf arrived at the prison expecting to visit his son. Instead he learned the news of Willi's execution, his remains misplaced, and his farewell letters lost. Another day, an envelope arrived at the Graf household, one addressed to Willi and now returned to the family. A single word on the envelope announced: "Deceased." It was months before Willi's family laid him to rest.

Anneliese would forever hear the echoes of Willi's last messages asking for remembrance and reassuring that others would carry the torch lit by the White Rose.

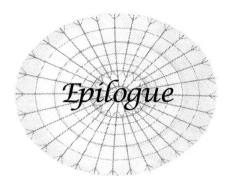

# Teachers' Meeting
# Munich, Germany
# August 13, 2003

THE EYE OF THE *LICHTHOF* stared down at me; its clear blue lens cast light into the courtyard of the Ludwig-Maximilians-University in Munich. At 10 o'clock on a Wednesday morning, we waited for our appointed meeting. The stairs, the hallways, the balconies, and the statuary of King Ludwig and Prince Leopold swirled around me—all pieces of the tragic drama that unfolded at this site on February 18, 1943. I imagined the rain of leaflets floating down from the balustrade, landing at my feet, and I wondered in what exact spot Hans and Sophie Scholl had stood when they were arrested.

I wandered up the staircase stopping for a moment at the statue of Doryphorus. Then deciding to turn right, I took a hundred paces down a long corridor lined on one side with graceful arched windows letting sun settle on the marble stone floor. For a moment, I sat in a window's alcove and examined the ornate doors of the *Grosse Aula* towering over me, and I envisioned student-soldiers like Alex, Willi, Hans, and Christoph, and women students like Sophie and Traute waiting for Professor Huber's lecture to begin. I wondered, too, which doorway hid the former Gestapo office, the first stop for Hans and Sophie at the beginning of their final ordeal that week in February.

Rounding the second level balconies, I traced the smooth gray and white-stoned rails leading me back to the coolness of the courtyard beneath a glass-domed ceiling that beckoned me to look upward and outward. My eye stopped at the entranceway to the *Grosser Hörsaal*, the *auditorium maximum*, where a gorgeous inlaid mosaic portrayed a green-gowned woman casting golden seeds like stars against an indigo sky. The words, *medicina, jurisprudentia, philosophia,* framed her portrait.

At the top of the central stairway, a man's figure appeared—first the shock of white hair, then the tall frame moving slowly down the steps, a gait suggesting an easy familiarity with these spaces. Finally in focus, we extended greetings and introductions to Franz Josef Müller, a White Rose associate. In 1942–43, he was then a teen-ager moved to help with the distribution of resistance leaflets. Now, the former history teacher, along with Anneliese Knoop-Graf, co-directed the White Rose Foundation housed in a space adjacent to the *Lichthof*. Herr Müller led us to a White Rose Memorial relief near the entry to the foundation's exhibit where he invited us to imagine this place in 1945, not long after the war's end, crowded with several hundred people, among them parents of White Rose members. He recalled the tears shed that day.

In the exhibition hall, Herr Müller gathered us around a conference table in the reference center where books about the White Rose and the Third Reich crammed the shelves. He suggested that White Rose members emerged from a milieu that fostered independent and democratic thinking. Then, perhaps because he knew he was speaking to teachers, he related how he and some other students could measure a teacher's enthusiasm for National Socialism. Teachers were expected to say, "Heil Hitler," but some lent only a limp, cursory hand as an excuse for a salute. He also recalled students clapping when teachers walked out after the appointment of a Nazi as new director of a school. From time to time Müller rose from his chair to dramatize a portion of his personal story or his commentary on resistance in general. Remembering, he leaned forward, squinting his eyes for emphasis.

Through a labyrinth of photo and poster displays, the director stopped at each station, noting the individuals portrayed. Sophie Scholl, he believed, could be considered the most powerful of the group. Represented in the display were Huber, Harnack, the Hirzels, Graf, Schmorell, Probst, and portraits of Ulm youths including Müller. Drawn to glass exhibit cases, my attention turned to the collection: Willi Graf's diary, his German/Russian songbook, the crucifix he carried on the Russian frontier, a suitcase that had transported leaflets from Ulm to Stuttgart, and a blouse embroidered by Sophie Scholl. These and other surviving objects testify to the truth of these individuals as ordinary human beings living in extraordinary circumstances.

After extending our appreciation for his time, I understood better what has kept Müller attached to this place at Ludwig-Maximilians-University. Even though he did have the opportunity to study in the United States after the war, he declined. His family and his home were in Germany. After the war, he had observed the transformation of some American soldiers to teachers in a program called the GYA, "German Youth Activity." In this process of denazification, particularly of Hitler Youth, young people were taught not to obey blindly but rather to discuss and ask questions. To educate rather than punish the youths, in Franz Müller's opinion, was an honorable idea.

We had yet another meeting in the *Lichthof*, scheduled for early afternoon. Before long, three teachers joined us from the Christoph-Probst-Gymnasium (CPG), a grade 5 through 13 school in Gilching. Several e-mails, faxes, and other transAtlantic communications had worked their magic and brought us to this moment. We greeted Peter Schubert and Robert Volkmann, both teachers and authors of a book about Christoph Probst: a chronicle in text, interviews, document, and photographs of the young family man tried and executed as a member of the White Rose. Accompanying them, Katrin

Stadlinger-Kessel, an English teacher at CPG, met us with enthusiasm and a warm smile. Later, we learned that in the 1950's, Katrin's family had lived on Emil-Dittler-Strasse in the very same house that had been Carl Muth's residence, the place where the Scholls and others were introduced to the "other Germany" in the house that protected an extensive forbidden library. The connection amazed me.

Months earlier while reviewing sources for my work, I discovered Robert and Peter's book through their school's web-site and was then able to order it for my collection. In his arti-cle, *"Christoph Probst—Das Leben eines Aufrechten,"* Herr Schubert reported that the school has borne Christoph's name since 1993, not only as a memorial to Probst but also as a reminder that the struggles for social justice continue. We learned the school has served as a meeting place, especially on the occasion of anniversaries, for surviving family members, among them Dr. Michael Probst, Christoph's son, as well as fel-low associates of the White Rose. Peter presented us with the school's 2002–2003 yearbook which brimmed with excitement recording the visit of Wolfgang Thierse, President of the Ger-man Parliament, who spoke at the school on February 18, 2003, marking the 60th anniversary of the capture, trial, and execu-tions of the Scholls and Christoph Probst. Gathered in the audi-torium of the Christoph-Probst-Gymnasium, the students and other guests heard his hard question: Why was there so little resistance? Then they followed as he discussed the Nazi's ideo-logical takeover, the dictatorship, and the "Einsicht," the insight and understanding that led to the White Rose resistant feelings. The Christoph-Probst-Gymnasium student yearbook celebrated art, music, student excursions to places like Poland, England, and Costa Rica, and a partnership with a school in India. This journal served as a testament to the school's global outreach and a mirror of President Thierse's further remarks about the importance of continued work for tolerance, democ-racy, and freedom in a pluralistic society bolstered by civil courage.

Our chatter in the *Lichthof* bounced off the walls in a cho-rus of echoes as we headed toward the exit of the university. At one last stop, our German hosts pointed to an inscription suggesting its informal translation as: *We will keep the memory of those who died in virtue.* It is a message considered by some as an indirect reference to the White Rose.

No sooner had we crossed busy Ludwigstrasse when a group of young men, former students of Peter, Robert, and Katrin, stopped for a brief exchange. On an earlier evening Bryon, our world language specialist, had told Karen, Ardith, and me that every language has a musicality to it. One can learn the vocabulary without the musicality, rhythm, stress and intonation, but real communication is complex. But the language of this encounter felt very familiar, the chance reunion when the "So good to see you," and the smiles are truly genuine. I recognized the universal language of teachers willing to be open and approachable to their students. It seemed appropriate to be standing near the street sign reading, "Professor-Huber-Platz."

Katrin, Peter, and Robert led us away from the university, providing historical commentary about the White Rose as we wove through the *Englischer Garten* where Sophie had celebrated her twenty-first birthday just months before her death and where Willi had cycled on solitary Sunday afternoons. Perhaps the youths had hoped to grow old here, sitting on a bench where little girls in red-checkered dresses with embroidered bodices picked bouquets of flowering weeds to give to grandmother or grandfather. It was also here that White Rose friendships and visions had germinated.

Now in 2003, the park nourished simple happiness— walking the dog, feeding the ducks, lying on the lawn, and running, jogging, or watching birds in flight as their white bellies reflected on the lake's surface. The teachers explained the park's landscape design as a counter reaction to conformity, following the patterns of the natural terrain, shaped in part by the Rivers Isar and Eisbach. As my colleague Karen later reflected, "There seems to be an instant bond between educators, even if there is a half a world separating the place where they fulfill this role." Her musings continued, "A side conversation between myself and Peter Schubert...as we walked from the University in Munich to the English Garden for lunch, revealed that we both have teenage sons who are "finding" themselves as they work their way through college." And so our relaxed conversations shifted as we talked history, family, culture, school, and food.

Arriving at the park's well-known beer garden, we chose a long table beneath a shade tree with a good view of the *Chinesischer Turm* (Chinese Tower). Nearly two o' clock, we gave in to our hunger, letting our new German friends advise and explain the array of choices served in the food pavilion. We talked about regional variations of the word for pretzel, took photos, and then turned our talk serious once again. I wondered how Christoph Probst's story was received by the students in their school. Robert admitted there are times when the students respond: No more Probst again, or times when his students feel Christoph's story is too far removed from their experiences. Katrin joined in, telling how her focus has been to prod her students to think critically about the dilemma of the White Rose members, particularly Christoph Probst's added concerns as the father of toddlers, and to engage students in open discussion. Later when Bryon asked Peter, "What is the worth of seeking after the truth of this story; how does it have any relevance to today?" Peter asserted that it is about taking a stand, though it does not have to be a political one.

We ended our lunch break with ceremonial gift-giving. For them, we had brought Caroline Kennedy's edited collection of Jacqueline Kennedy's favorite poems. Katrin happily announced she would use the volume with her English classes. We each received a copy of their beautiful book, "...damit Deutschland weiterlebt" Christoph Probst 1919–1943, a copy of the school yearbook, and a large bag full of what every teacher loves, resources and ideas. They understood, as we did, that the story of the White Rose needs the continued discipline of research and refinement, and that as new, heretofore unavailable documents surface, the narrative will clarify and deepen. As Peter pointed out, documents related to the White Rose, earlier held in East Germany had only become available after 1989.

It appears of great interest to the Probst family that research and scholarship continues. In 2003, Herta, her son Dr.

Michael Probst, and her grandson, posed for a photo taken at the White Rose Institute, along with Professor Wolfgang Huber, Kurt Huber's son, and Erich Schmorell, Alex Schmorell's brother, and four other relatives and associates of the White Rose. The institute has organized itself to broaden the scope of White Rose studies through scholarly research. It also provides academic lectures dedicated to workshops examining issues such as right-wing radicalism and its threats against democratic systems. A more recent lecture in 2006 examined a question related to the causes of hostility toward the "other," and the socio-emotional profile of youths prone to antipathy toward the stranger in their midst.

Our hosts graciously obliged when I asked to visit Franz-Josef-Strasse 13 where Sophie and Hans had lived at the time of their arrest. Because he had a late afternoon appointment, Robert said farewell, and the rest of us set out towards the streets of Schwabing. We strolled the winding paths again, glad for the shade trees and the sound of water rushing beneath the footpath's stone-walled culverts. Making our exit from the *Englischer Garten,* we entered a neighborhood once a bohemian student and artists' quarters, but now a stately collection of gentrified buildings, well-kept and renovated. Many were several stories high with shiny glass transoms topping heavy wooden doors trimmed in colorful and decorative molding. In contrast, bicycles leaned against a non-descript beige concrete building at Franz-Josef-Strasse 13, clearly a worn, post-war construction. The façade flashed graffiti spray-painted in blues, browns, and green. A grey stone slab affixed to the house identified the Scholl siblings' association with this address.

"It must be here in the back," Peter moved toward a passage driveway.

"I think so," I knew the secret meetings and the leaflet production sometimes took place in the Scholls' apartment in the Garden House behind the main building at #13. I had imagined a little house, but the residence was a large, sturdy structure well hidden from the road. We circled in the passageway observing from a distance so as not to disturb the current residents. A welcome breeze carried our conversation away and swept tree branches along the portico bearing the insignia of a white flower above the green door. I could picture the youths in 1943 leaving with suitcase and briefcase crammed with leaflets, determined and committed to the message they carried.

My fellow traveler Ardith would later write her own reflections of our pilgrimage, "I have stood there. I have spoken with Germans. I have seen places that some are only able to learn about in books. I feel connected with the people of Germany, the history of Germany, and the future of Germany in a way that would never have been possible without the help of the Geraldine R. Dodge Foundation."

Turning from the passageway, our presence drew the attention of a man from the neighboring building. Recognizing our interest in the history of the place, he pointed out a mailbox bearing the name Todt. The German teachers were as interested in hearing his comments as we were. Strangely, this was the site of the former residence of Dr. Fritz Todt, the director of the construction of the autobahn project and for the Zeppelin Field arena. Todt had been a speaker at the party day rally in 1936, just at the time Hans Scholl's enthusiasm for the Hitler cult began to wane. We were all surprised by the serendipitous encounter with this man and the juxtaposition of the two sites.

Leaving Franz-Josef-Strasse in the late afternoon, our hosts did not have to convince us to stop for the best iced-coffee in Munich at a sidewalk café on Leopoldstrasse where cars, vans, and motorcycles whizzed down an avenue lined with towering trees. Talk drifted again to curriculum matters. Frequently students from Christoph-Probst-Gymnasium travel to Dachau, just twelve miles outside Munich, Katrin and Peter reported. Annually, a Holocaust survivor speaks to students as a living witness to the horrors of the Third Reich. Though we did not visit the school's campus that day in August, we later did see photos of a bronze statue of Christoph Probst that holds a place of honor in its foyer. It is the work of an art teacher, Brigitte Renner. An adjoining exhibit displays a collage formed in the shape of a rose, each petal expressing in words, design, and photo, student articulation of the Reich's deceptions and Christoph Probst's response.

"I will never forget Peter, Robert, and Katrin," Ardith later commented. "They generously gave of their time, their friendship, and their knowledge of Munich as well as the White Rose...We could have spent days talking about the White Rose, sharing stories, and ideas on education, and philosophizing with them."

During our time together, Katrin had explained a school tradition clearly showing that honoring the White Rose continues to be upheld and deeply felt when fifth graders on their first day of school at the Christoph-Probst-Gymnasium are handed a single white rose. This tribute, rich in sentiment, holds the promise of instilling in young people the courage, compassion, and determination that characterized all of the members of the White Rose and those associated with them. At the beginning of my next school year, I found myself imagining once again that moment when the German teachers greet their new students with the symbolic white rose. Our journey to the White Rose in Germany continued to transform us. Karen mused that in preparing for our trip, she had translated a German phrase, "that my father would speak—*'verstehen Sie nicht?'*—which I always knew to mean, 'Understand?' Yes, I was beginning to understand a lot of things more clearly."

As author Aharon Appelfeld has written, the view was turning from collective to individualized, observing people, places and events in the biographies of unique human beings, both from the past and in the present. Our teacher meetings had come to a close. In just two days, our experiences powerfully confirmed the graffiti messages splashed on the walls of Munich's buildings after the first White Rose executions: *Their spirit lives.*

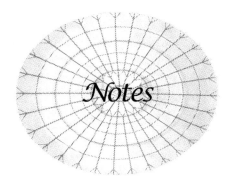

# Notes

(The number in parentheses refers to the appropriate bibliography entry.)

**Prologue: Teachers' Meeting, Crailsheim, Germany, 2003**
Gerhard Frank's mural can be viewed on the Geschwister-Scholl-Schule, Crailsheim, Germany website: <http://www.gss.scha.schule-bw.de>.

"Judith und Lisa waren…" Reuter. **(79)**

The account of the August 11, 2003 meeting in Crailsheim, Germany is based on the author's journal and notes as well as video recordings of conversations with Ute Nettlau, Harry Nettlau, Manfred Hügelmaier, Joachim Scharr, Ursula Scharr, and including Morris County Teacher Fellowship Reports of Ardith Collins, Bryon Pinajian, Karen Orlando, and Ruth Bernadette Melon **(69)**

"moral compass" Fogelman 38. **(33)**

**Chapter 1 "Blood Brotherhood"**

"Be faithful, be Pure, Be German." Gavin, "Hitler Youth: Timeline and Organizational Info." **(38)**

"Praise Be to..." "Hitler's Youth, "Molded." (50)

"One State, One People, One Leader." Furman 63. (34)

**Chapter 2 "Subversion**

"Germany Awake! Judah Perish!" Furman 63. (34)

**Chapter 3 "Saboteurs"**

"saboteurs of German unity" Walker 99. (96)

"Intelligence beasts with..." Furman 61. (34)

"...always speak the truth..." *Katholischer* in Walker 99. (58)

**Chapter 4 "Allegiances"**

"I swear by..." Hanser 153. (48)

"Those of the same..." United States Holocaust Memorial Museum. "Anchluss Introduction Articles April 1938."(88)

**Chapter 5 "Solitude"**

*"Kinder, Kirsche, Kyche"* "Women and Girls Under Nazi Rule." (103)

**Chapter 6 "Alliances"**

"She instilled in us..." Page. JCC Lecture. (73)

"unproductive national comrades." Gavin, "Cardinal Galen's Speech Against Nazi Euthanasia." (36)

"...the search for truth..." "Casper Welcomes..." (15)

"Blood and Honor." Gavin. "Hitler Youth: Prelude to War." (37)

**Chapter 7 "Resolutions"**

"...separation and further treatment..." United States Holocaust Memorial Museum."Kiev and Babi Yar." (90)

"We have to do..." "Probst in English." Christoph-Probst-Gymnasium. (76)

*Concepts of Leaflet of the White Rose I.* This section represents this author's (RBM) summary highlighting key

concepts of the first message. It is presented in the context of this account in order for the reader to appreciate
the chronology of the thought development expressed in
the handbills and to more easily follow their evolution.
Several sources contain a record of the original leaflets
in German and/or English, as appendices in those texts.
These resources are listed in the Bibliography (60, 84,
and 24)

Chapter 9 "Conscience"

*Concepts of Leaflet of the White Rose II, III, IV.* As with the
first leaflet, the next three are conceptually presented in
the text. These are this author's (RBM) summaries highlighting focal points of each. The concentration of these
summaries within a few chapters reflects the pace at
which these handbills were produced. Summaries only
appear again after a considerable break, again reflecting
the pause in leaflet composition and distribution and the
reasons for it.

Chapter 10 "Departures"

"July 22, 1942. Today…" Berg 171. (9)

"beasts" Berg, 169. (9)

"Himmelfahrstrasse" Gilbert 398. (44)

Chapter 11 "Brutality"

"We only have to kick…" *In the Wolf's Lair, Leben von Adolf
Hitler.* (53)

"Close your hearts…" *In the Wolf's Lair, Leben von Adolf Hitler.*
(53)

Chapter 12 "Resistance"

"Guns Before Butter" *In the Wolf's Lair, Leben von Adolf Hitler.*
(53)

"I think as I please…" "Die Gedenken Sind Frei" (20)

"We are Barbarians…" *In the Wolf's Lair, Leben von Adolf Hitler.*
(53)

## Chapter 13 "Circulation"

*Concepts of Leaflet of the Resistance (the fifth handbill).* This constitutes this author's (RBM) conceptual summary and highlights of the fifth handbill.

"last man and last round" In the Wolf's Lair, Leben von Adolf Hitler. **(53)**

## Chapter 14 "Writing on the Wall"

*Concepts of Christoph Probst's draft called "Stalingrad!"* This segment represents this author's (RBM) conceptual summary and highlights of a draft written by Christoph Probst.

*Concepts of the sixth Leaflet, "Students!"* This segment reflects this author's (RBM) conceptual summary and highlights of the sixth and final leaflet. All of this author's summaries are based on a reading of translations of the original documents.

## Chapter 16 "A Higher Court"

"He is not dead…" "Memories and Reminiscences of Christoph Probst." **(66)**

## Chapter 17 "Convictions"

"Nothing is possible unless…" "Hitler's Youth Delusion." **(49)**

## Chapter 18 "To Life"

"The victory of Kursk…" "End of WW2 in Europe." History Channel. **(29)**

"I know that my Redeemer Liveth" Handel. *Messiah.* **(47)**

"but we shall all be changed…" Handel. *Messiah.* **(47)**

## Epilogue

The account of the August 13, 2003 meeting in Munich, Germany is based on the author's journal and notes as well as video recordings of conversations with Franz-Josef-Müller, Robert Volkmann, Peter Schubert, Katrin Stadlinger-Kessel, including Morris County Teacher Fellowship Reports of Ardith Collins, Bryon Pinajian, Karen Orlando, and Ruth Bernadette Melon. **(69)**

**Photographs by**
Ardith Collins and Ruth Bernadette Melon

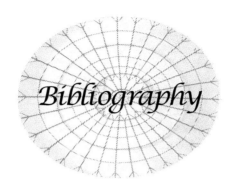

# Bibliography

1.  Aicher-Scholl, Inge. *Sippenhaft*. Frankfurt am Main: S. Fischer, 1993.

2.  "Appeal to the Catholic Youth." *Volkischer Beobachter*. March 1934, quoted in Lawrence D. Walker, *Hitler Youth and Catholic Youth 1933–1936: A Study in Totalitarian Conquest*. Washington, D.C.: The Catholic Press, 1970.

3.  Appelfeld, Aharon. "Individualization of the Holocaust." Translated from Hebrew by G. Green. Ben Gurion University in *Holocaust Chronicles: Individualizing the Holocaust Through Diaries and Other Contemporaneous Personal Accounts* edited by Robert Moses Shapiro.Hoboken, New Jersey: KTAV Publishing House, Inc.

4.  "Archiv Der Stadt Linz." *Digital City*. <http://.linz.at/archiv.html>.

5.  Ascherson, Neal. *The World at War: Inside the Third Reich—Germany 1940–1944*. USA: Thames Television, 1982, Videocassette.

6. *Baedeker's Germany*. Translated by James Hogarth, Englewood Cliffs, New Jersey: Prentice-Hall, Inc. (Originally published in German as *Baedeker Stuttgart*).

7. Baez-Graf, Mathilde. "It Was Not Fun and Games." Willi-Graf-Realschule. <http://home.t-online.de.willi-graf-realschule/home.htm> (accessed October 11, 2001).

8. Bartoletti, Susan Campbell. *Hitler Youth: Growing up in Hitler's Shadow*. New York: Scholastic Inc., 2005.

9. Berg, Mary. *Warsaw Ghetto: A Diary by Mary Berg*. ed. S.L. Shneiderman. New York: L.B. Fischer, 1945.

10. "Bonhoeffer, Agent of Grace: The Film" <http://www.pbs.org/opb/bonhoeffer/film/plot.html> (accessed January 6, 2002).

11. Borzykowski, Tuvia. *Between Tumbling Walls*. Tel Aviv, 1972, 1976. Excerpts in *The Holocaust: A History of the Jews of Europe During the Second World War* by Martin Gilbert. New York: Henry Holt and Company, 1985.

12. Browning, Robert. *The Pied Piper of Hamelin*. Illustrated by Kate Greenaway. London, England: Frederick Warne and Co., Ltd., 1888.

13. Brysac, Shareen Blair. *Resisting Hitler: Mildred Harnack and the Red Orchestra*. New York: Oxford University Press, 2000.

14. Carroll, James. "The Holocaust and the Catholic Church." *Atlantic On-line*. October. <http://www.theatlantic.com/issues/990ct/9119pope2.htm> (accessed September 20, 2001).

15. "Casper Welcomes New Students, Parents to Stanford." Stanford University News Service. September 25, 1995. <http://www.stanford.edu/dept/news> (accessed March 1, 2006).

16. Chaussy, Ulrich and Franz Josef Müller. *The White Rose: The Resistance by Students Against Hitler 1942–43*. Munich: White Rose Foundation, 1991.

17. "Clement Augustus Cardinal Count of Galen." <http://www.damascenus.tripod.com> (accessed October 21, 2001).

18. "Concordat." Microsoft Encarta Online Encyclopedia 2001. <http://encarta.msn.com>.

19. Dekel, Sheila Cohn and Lucette Matalon Lagnado. *Children of the Flame: Dr. Josef Mengele and the Untold Story of the Twins of Auschwitz.* New York: William Morrow & Co., Inc., 1991.

20. "Die Gedenken Sind Frei," a German folksong. Translated by Arthur Kevess and Gerda Lerner. <http://www.jlrweb.com/whiterose/free/html>.

21. Diehn, Karen. "Traute Lafrenz." Biography. *Politisch Verfolgte in Hamburg 1933–1945.* Ein Projekt Der Arbeitsstelle Für Hamburgische Geschichte. <webapp.rrz.uni-hamburg.de/~mmpl/mmpl/bio/bio.php?id=3> (accessed 2006).

22. Distel, Barbara. *Dachau Concentration Camp.* Haerne, Bruxelles: Comité International de Dachau, 1972.

23. Dumbach, Annette E. and Jud Newborn. *Shattering the German Night: The Story of the White Rose.* Boston: Little, Brown and Company, 1986.

24. Dumbach, Annette E. and Jud Newborn. *Sophie Scholl & the White Rose.* Oxford: Oneworld Publications, 2006. (Originally published as *Shattering the German Night: The Story of the White Rose.* Boston: Little, Brown and Company, 1986).

25. Dvorson, Alexa. *The Hitler Youth: March Toward Madness.* New York: Rosen Publishing Group, Inc., 1999.

26. "The Early German Youth Movement." *The German Youth Movement.* <http://www.bruderhof.com/youth/> (accessed August 8, 2001).

27. Eckert, Hans und Anneliese Knoop-Graf. *Gedenkschrift zum 50. Jahrestag der Hinrichtung des Saarbrücker Widerstandkämpfers Willi Graf.* Saarbrücken: Landeshauptstadt, 1993.

28. Edeiken, Yale F. "Introduction to the Einsatzgruppen." <http://www.holocaust-history.org/intro-einsatz/> (accessed September 5, 2001).

29. "End of World War Two in Europe." *History Channel*. October 2002. <http://www.historychannel.com>.

30. Erickson, John. *Road to Berlin: Stalin's War with Germany Vol. 2*. London: Weidenfeld & Nicholson, 1983.

31. Fackenheim, Emil. *To Mend the World*. New York: Schocken Books, 1983.

32. Fermi, Laura. *Illustrious Immigrants: The Intellectual Migration from Europe 1930–1941*. Chicago and London: University of Chicago Press, 1968.

33. Fogelman, Eva. *Conscience and Courage: Rescuers of Jews During the Holocaust*. New York: Anchor Books, 1994.

34. Furman, Harry, ed. *The Holocaust and Genocide: A Search for Conscience, an Anthology for Students*. New York: Anti-Defamation League of B'nai B'rith, 1983.

35. Garten Der Frauen, e.V. "Die Frauen: Erna Stahl, Reformpädagogin und Schulleiterin." <http://garten-der-frauen.de/gedenk.html#stahl>.

36. Gavin, Philip, ed. "Cardinal Clemens von Galen Against Nazi Euthanasia." *The History Place: Great Speeches Collection*. <http://www.historyplace.com/speeches/galen.htm>.

37. ___. "Hitler Youth: Prelude to War 1933–1938." *History Place* <http://www.historyplace.com/worldwar2/hitleryouth/>.

38. ___."Hitler Youth: Timeline and Organizational Info." *History Place*. <http://www.historyplace.com/worldwar2/hitleryouth/hj-timeline.htm>.

39. ___. "Holocaust Timeline: Nuremberg Race Laws." *History Place*.   <http://www.historyplace.com/worldwar2/holocaust/h-nurem-laws.htm>.

40. Gebel, Hans-Josef. *Willi Graf, ein Lebensbild. Zum 40. Jahrestag seiner Hinrichtung am 12.October 1943*, in, *Zeitschrift für die Geschichte de Saargegend* Jg.31, 1983.

41. "German Pre-War Expansion." United States Holocaust Memorial Museum. <htpp://www.ushmm.com>. (accessed October 3, 2001).

42. *Gestapo Interrogation Transcripts: Willi Graf, Alexander Schmorell, Hans Scholl, and Sophie Scholl. ZC13267, Volumes 1–16.* Translated by Ruth Sachs. Phoenixville, Pennsylvania USA: Exclamation! Publishers, 2002–2003.

43. *Gestapo Interrogation Transcripts: Willi Graf, Alexander Schmorell, Hans Scholl, and Sophie Scholl. NJ1704, Volumes 1–33.* Translated by Ruth Sachs. Phoenixville, Pennsylvania USA: Exclamation! Publishers, 2002–2003.

44. Gilbert, Martin. *The Holocaust: A History of the Jews of Europe During the Second World War.* New York: Henry Holt and Company, 1985.

45. Gill, Anton. *An Honourable Defeat.* New York: Henry Holt & Company, 1994.

46. Goebbels, Josef. "Nation Rise Up, and Let the Storm Break Loose." In *German Propaganda Archive.* (Originally published as "Nun, Volk steh auf, und Sturm brich los! Rede im Berliner Sportpalast," *Der steile Aufstieg.* Munich: Zentralverlag der NSDAP. 1944). < http://www.calvin.edu/academic/cas/gpa/goeb36.htm>.

47. Handel. "I know that my Redeemer liveth." *Messiah.* *Wikipedia: The Free Encyclopedia.* <http://en.wikipedia.org/wiki/Messiah_ (Handel)>. (accessed July 6, 2006).

48. Hanser, Richard. *A Noble Treason: The Revolt of the Munich Students Against Hitler.* New York: G.P. Putnam's Sons, 1979.

49. "Hitler's Youth: Delusion." *Australia: A & E Network,* 2000. Television broadcast viewed October 26, 2000.

50. "Hitler's Youth: Molded." *Australia: A & E Network,* 2000. Television broadcast viewed October 26, 2000.

51. Hölderlin, Frederich. "When I Was a Boy," "Bread and Wine," and "Homecoming." Translated by James Mitchell in *The Fire of the Gods Drives Us to Set Forth by Day and by Night.* San

Francisco, California: Hoddtpoll Press, 1978. accessed at <http://home.att.net/~holderlin>.

52. Huch, Ricarda. "Obituary of Willi Graf." *Metamorphosis*, 1948.      <http://www.home.t-online.de/home/willi-graf-realschule>. (accessed October10, 2001).

53. *In the Wolf's Lair: Leben von Adolf Hitler*. Produced by Robert Kruger, narrated by Robert Neumann. Europa Film, 1961. Videocassette.

54. *Jahresbericht Christoph-Probst-Gymnasium Gilching* (Yearbook) Gilching: CPG, 2002–2003.

55. Janson, H.W. and Anthony F. Janson. *History of Art*, 5th edition revised. Joanne Greenspan, ed. New York: Harry N. Abrams, Inc., 1997.

56. Jens, Inge, ed. *At the Heart of the White Rose: Letters and Diaries of Hans and Sophie Scholl*. Translated by J. Maxwell Brownjohn. New York: Harper and Row, 1987. (Originally published as *Hans, Sophie Scholl, Briefe und Aufzeichnungen*. Frankfurt am Main: S. Fischer, 1984).

57. *Joseph Schultz*. Directed by Predag Golubvic. A Zastava Film. Wombat Productions, Inc., 1973. Videocassette.

58. *Katholischer Jungmännerverband.Reg.*51, pp146–147 translated and quoted in *Hitler Youth and Catholic Youth 1933–1936: A Study in Totalitarian Conquest* by Lawrence D. Walker. Washington, D.C.: The Catholic University of America Press, 1970.

59. Knoop-Graf, Anneliese und Inge Jens. *Willi Graf Briefe und Aufzeichnungen*. Frankfurt am Main: S. Fischer, 1988.

60. "Leaflets of the White Rose." Texts of the leaflets in English. <http://www.jlrweb.com.whiterose>.

61. *Letters to Freya 1939–1945: Helmuth James von Moltke*. Edited and translated from the German by Beate Ruhm von Oppen. New York: Alfred A. Knopf, 1990.

62. Lipp, Wolfgang. *Guide to Ulm Cathedral*. Translated by John R. Weinlick and Michael Foster, sixth edition. Ulm: Vaas Verlag, 1997.

63. Melon, Ruth Bernadette. "Sixty Years After the White Rose: Their Spirit Lives." Paper presented at the 33rd Annual Scholars' Conference on the Holocaust and the Churches, Philadelphia, March 2003. Annual Scholar's Conference CD-ROM, 2003.

64. ___."Their Spirit Lives: A Journey to the White Rose in Germany." *Perspectives on the Holocaust* 8, no.1 (fall 2004): 6–7, 16. A Publication of the Drew University Center for Holocaust/Genocide Studies. Madison, New Jersey.

65. ___. "Voices of the White Rose." Master's thesis, Goucher College. Baltimore, Maryland, 2002.

66. Memories and Reminiscences of Christoph Probst." Christoph-Probst-Gymnasium, Gilching. <http://www.gpg-gilching.de> Translated for this author by Bill Ruff. Whippany, New Jersey. (accessed October 1, 2001).

67. "Mildred Harnack and the Red Orchestra—Cast of Characters." <http://www.mildredharnack.com/cast.html> (accessed February 2, 2002).

68. Moll, Christine. "The White Rose in Light of New Archival Evidence." In *Resistance Against the Third Reich 1933–1990*. Michael Geyer and John W. Boyer, eds. Distributed for University of Chicago Press Journals, 1992, 1994.

69. *Morris County Teacher Fellowships Reports: 2003 Cohort.* Morristown, New Jersey: Geraldine R. Dodge Foundation, 2004.

70. Mozal, Harry W., "Trial of the Major War Criminals before the International Military Tribunal at Nuremberg. Blue Series," Vol. 1, P317–18, "von Schirach." *The Holocaust History Project.* < http://www.holocaust-history.org/works/imt/01/htm/t317.htm>.

71. "Nazi Conspiracy and Aggression." Vol. 1, Chapter VII. *Means Used by the Nazi Conspirators in Gaining Control of the German State* (Part 45 of 55). <http://www.nizkor.org> (accessed July 2, 2001).

72. Owings, Alison. *Frauen: German Women Recall the Third Reich.* New Brunswick, New Jersey: Rutgers University Press, 1993.

73  Page, Traute Lafrenz. Metrowest Jewish Community Center (JCC) lecture. West Orange, New Jersey. February 4, 2006.

74. Photo Archives. Hessisches Hauptstaatsarchiv, courtesy of the United States Holocaust Memorial Museum. <http://www.ushmm.org> (accessed October 2001).

75. "Principal Feasts of the Year." *Roman Missal*. New York: The Regina Press, 1936.

76. "Probst in English." Christoph-Probst-Gymnasium,Gilching, Germany. <http://www.cpg-gilching.de> (accessed September 25, 2001).

77. Rempel, Gerhard. *Hitler's Children: The Hitler Youth and the SS*. Chapel Hill: The University of North Carolina Press, 1989.

78. Rentschler, Eric. "Emotional Engineering: Hitler Youth Quex." *Modernism/Modernity* 2:3. The Hopkins University Press, 1995.

79. Reuter, Elisabeth. *Best Friends*. Germany: Yellow Brick Road Press, 1993. (Originally published in German under the title: *Judith and Lisa*. München: Verlag Heinrich Ellerman, 1988).

80. Roland, Charles G. *Courage Under Siege: Disease, Starvation, and Death in the Warsaw Ghetto*. New York: Oxford University Press, 1992. Excerpts from Chapter 6, pp 99–104. "Scenes of Hunger and Starvation." *Remember.org—A Cybrary of the Holocaust*, 1995.<http://remember.org/courage/chapter6.html> (accessed December 13, 2001).

81. Rothmund, Marc, director, and Fred Breinersdorfer, writer. *Sophie Scholl, The Final Days (Sophie Scholl Die Letzten Tage)* New York release: February 17, 2006.

82. Ryan, Peter. *Interview with George J. Wittenstein*. Santa Barbara, California: Bay Area Holocaust Oral History Project, November 23, 1996. Tapes 1–4.

83. Sachs, Ruth. *White Rose History: Volume 1: Coming Together: January 31, 1933-April 30, 1942, The Unfinished Story*. Phoenixville, Pennsylvania: Exclamation! Publishers, 2002.

84. Scholl, Inge. *The White Rose: Munich 1942–1943*. Translated by Arthur R. Schultz. Hanover, New Hampshire: Wesleyan

Press, 1983. (Originally published as *Das Weisse Rose*. Frankfurt am Main: Verlag der Frankfurter Hefte GmbH, 1952).

85. Stefan Zweig Collection. Daniel A. Reed Library, New York. <http://fredonia.edu/library/zweig.htm>. (accessed March 31, 2001).

86. *The Third White Rose Trial, July 13, 1943: Eickemeyer, Söhngen, Dohrn, and Geyer.* Translated by Ruth Sachs. Phoenixville, Pennsylvania USA: Exclamation! Publishers, 2002–2003.

87. Tillich, Paul. "A Guiding Light in the Darkness of the New Year, December 1942." in *Against the Third Reich: Paul Tillich's Wartime Radio Broadcasts into Nazi Germany.* Edited by Ronald H. Stone and Matthew Lon Weaver. Translated by Matthew Lon Weaver. Louisville, Kentucky: Westminster John Knox Press: 1998.

88. United States Holocaust Memorial Museum. "Anchluss Introduction Articles April 1938." <http://www.ushmm.com>.

89. United States Holocaust Memorial Museum. "German Resistance to Hitler." *Holocaust Encyclopedia.* <http://www.ushmm.com/wlc/article.jsp?ModuleId=10005208> (accessed December 11, 2001).

90. United States Holocaust Memorial Museum. "Kiev and Babi Yar." *Holocaust Encyclopedia.*<http://ushmm.org/wlc/en/index.php?ModuleId=10005421&type=normal+article> (accessed October 31, 2001).

91. Verhoeven, Michael, director, *The White Rose*, the film. Collector's Edition, Color, Subtitled, 1981. Videocassette.

92. Vieregg, Hildegard. u.a.(Hrsg): *Willi Graf Jugend im Nationalsozialismus im Spiegel von Briefen, Gruppe Willi Graf im Bund Neudeutschland.* München, 1984. Portions translated for this author by Bill Ruff. Whippany, New Jersey, 2001.

93. Vinke, Hermann. *The Short Life of Sophie Scholl*, Translated by Hedwig Pacher. USA: Harper & Row, 1984. (Originally published as *Das kurz Leben der Sophie Scholl*. Germany: Otto Maier Verlag Ravensburg, 1980).

94. Volkmann, Robert, Peter Schubert and Gernot Eschrich. *"...damit Deutschland weiterlebt": Christoph Probst 1919–1943.* Gilching, Germany: Christoph-Probst-Gymnasium, 2000.

95. von Olfers, Sibylle. *When the Root Children Wake Up.* Edinburgh: Floris Books, 1990. (Originally published in Germany as *Etwas von den Wurzelkindern,* 1906).

96. Walker, Lawrence D. *Hitler Youth and Catholic Youth 1933–1936: A Study in Totalitarian Conquest.* Washington, D.C.: The Catholic University Press, 1970.

97. "The Warsaw Ghetto." BBC Television. From a November 1940, SS cameraman's documentary for Himmler's personal album. Videocassette.

98. Weisse Rose Institut e.V. Leopoldstr.80802 Munich. < http://weisserose.info/>.

99. White Rose Foundation. Munich: Ludwig-Maximilians-University. <http://www.weisse-rose-stiftung.de>.

100. "Willi Graf: Fotogalerie." Willi-Graf-Realschule in Euskirchen, Germany. <http://home.t-online.de.willi-graf-realschule/home.htm>.

101. Wittenstein, George J. "The White Rose: German Youth Resistance to Hitler." In *Soundings: Collections of the University Library* XXII, no.28 (1991) Donald E. Fitch, ed. Santa Barbara, California: Graham Mackintosh University Library.

102. "Women Against Hitler." (*"de Frauen gegen Hitler"*). *Politik und Zeitgeschhehen ZDF.* <www.huete.t-online.de>.

103. "Women and Girls Under Nazi Rule." *Anne Frank in the World 1929–1945, Teacher Workbook, Utah Education Network.* <htpp://www.uen.org/annefrank/womenGirls.shtml>. (accessed October 10, 2001).

104. Ziegler, Armin. "Sophies Wissen." *Weisse-Rose-Studien.* <http://www.weisse-rose-studien.de.> (accessed March 13, 2006).

105. ___. "William Geyer; Eugene Grimminger." <http://www.lebensbilder.de>.

106. Zweig, Stefan. *The Tide of Fortune: Twelve Historical Miniatures*. Translated by Eden and Cedar Paul. New York: The Viking Press, 1940. (Originally published in Germany as *Sternstunden Der Menschheit*, 1927).

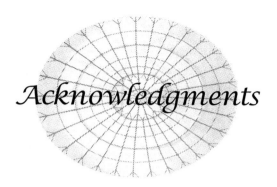

# Acknowledgments

The rhythms of the writing life set in motion, and my colleagues, family, and friends responded in countless supportive ways. Thanks to the Rockaway Township Public Schools in New Jersey for the gift of time. A sabbatical year allowed me to immerse myself in research, a catalyst for this project.

Praise and thanks to Leslie Rubinkowski, Phil Gerard, Paul Wilkes, and Tom French, my Goucher College mentors, whose generosity of spirit, expertise, and talents guided me through the process of writing a MFA manuscript that laid the foundation for this book.

Appreciation goes out to my never-distant Goucher classmates. Many offered feedback and critical readings of first drafts.

Jacqueline Berke, co-director of the Drew University Center for Holocaust and Genocide Studies, agreed to be my mentor as I wrote the last chapters when I entered the D.Litt program at Drew University. Her insight, editorial talents, and her enthusiasm for this project strengthened my will to move forward. She deserves my sincere thanks.

Additional thanks go to the Drew University community and particularly the Drew University Center for Holocaust/Genocide Study Publications for allowing me to name this volume from a portion of the title, "Their Spirit Lives: A Journey to the White Rose in Germany," an account of our trip to Germany, published in the Fall 2004 issue of *Perspectives on the Holocaust.*

Special appreciation is extended to the Geraldine R. Dodge Foundation for a fellowship grant enabling my teacher travel team to journey to Germany. Without their financial support and respect for the teaching profession, the special perspective of this book would not have materialized.

It is a rare gift to have individuals willing to say "yes" to another's vision and dream. My fellow teachers: Karen Orlando, Bryon Pinajian and Ardith Collins blessed me with that gift. Their companionship and their contributions to this White Rose project created a bond that will remain close to my heart.

Kudos again for Karen—for her patience, generosity, and outstanding technical support.

To our fellow teachers and associates in Germany: Ute Nettlau, Harry Nettlau, Manfred Hügelmaier, Joachim Scharr, Ursula Scharr, Peter Schubert, Robert Volkmann and Katrin-Stadlinger-Kessel, I send grateful regards. I thank them for answering the call "across the pond," for opening their hearts, minds, and their world. It was through them that we came to understand that the spirit of the White Rose does live still.

Thank you to the White Rose Foundation in Munich for their time and commentary at Ludwig-Maximilians-University.

Sincere thanks to Bill Ruff for his generous translations.

Heartfelt gratitude and thanks to Donald R. Ferrell for keeping watch and listening.

To my extended family, I send thanks for their continued interest and encouragement.

Love and thanks to my daughter Rebecca—ready to pour raspberry tea and dance in celebration. She challenged me when it all seemed too difficult: Know the stuff you're made of, Mom. Her grace, loving-kindness, and insight and Brian's car-ing, compassion, and love of nature will serve well those who cross their paths.

Love and thanks to my son David—ready to organize my files, prod me through a computerized world, and to discourse about the mysteries of the universe. Fond memories of phone calls from the labs, the libraries, and the train stations. His determination, skill, and creativity along with Jennifer's optimism and vitality will bless those who feel the touch of their healing arts.

Love and admiration to my husband Ira. His devotion and endless editorial readings of this book have been especially appreciated. He has been my companion through moments of despair and glimpses of joy in our work for Tikkun Olam.

# Guidelines for Reading Circles

This map of the *Journey to the White Rose in Germany* will guide readers or groups of readers in an exploration and discussion of the people, places, and events of the story. It suggests how attention might be focused so that questions arise organically from the group or individual facilitators.

**Part One** spans Chapters 1–5, taking the story back to the early 1930's and the decade preceding the flowering of the White Rose. Time moves in years. In each chapter, one or two of the focus characters, other than Professor Kurt Huber, is developed—Hans Scholl, Willi Graf, Alexander Schmorell, Christoph Probst, and Sophie Scholl. In each case, conflicts arise which become catalysts for the evolution of attitudes resistant to totalitarianism. The chapter titles reflect the struggles and responses the youths encountered—Blood Brotherhood, Subversion, Saboteurs, Allegiances, Solitude.

## Suggestions for organizing reading circle interaction:

**1.** Begin with the group or individuals responding to the chapter titles in a free association manner, gathering thoughts related to the concept in general and then bringing concentration into the context of Germany, the Third Reich, and WW2, and moving, if so desired, into associations made with the present day.

2.  Group members might decide to each follow more closely the biography, issues and events surrounding a particular character (Hans, Alex etc.) and bring into discussion the specific perspective of that individual. Each member of the circle may also conduct a search for photographs of that individual to bring to the group. German schools named for members of the White Rose generally have pictures posted on the web sites. For example, for Willi Graf photos go to "Willi Graf: Fotogalerie." Willi-Graf-Realschule in Euskirchen, Germany. <http://www.home.t-online.de.willi-graf-realschule/home.htm>.

**Digressions:** Interwoven throughout the narrative are significant digressions placing the White Rose persons and events in an historical and sociological context. Such digressions in Part One are listed below as a quick reference for further independent research.

**Chapter 1 "Blood Brotherhood":** The history and development of youth groups in Germany in the early 20th century; Baldur von Schirach, the twenty-six-year-old leader of the Hitler Youth turns a party group into the exclusive state youth group; Banned books; Hitler's rise to power; Social and economic conditions in Germany 1900–1945.

**Chapter 2 "Subversion":** The competition for power, jurisdiction, and status between the Gestapo and the Wehrmacht.

**Chapter 3 "Saboteurs":** Concordat between Hitler and the Catholic Church and how it protected Catholic youth until 1936; Nazi Party members who were Roman Catholics.

**Chapter 4 "Allegiances":** Hitler and the Treaty of Versailles; the Anschluss; the battle for France.

**Chapter 5 "Solitude":** St. Augustine; Novalis; Nazi efforts to create a state religion; Work service; Role and status of women in the Third Reich.

**Part Two** spans Chapters 6–11 This section chronicles the intersection of the youths' lives as medical student-soldiers (except for Sophie) in Munich, the formation of friendships based on common interests in the arts, sports, shared academic classes, military obligations, and finally the recognition of shared objections to the strangulation of civil liberties and basic human rights under the Third Reich. A philosophy and musicology professor, Kurt Huber, responds to the youths' appeal. Chapter titles reflect this progression of the story: Alliances, Resolution, Convergence, Conscience, Departures and Brutality.

In Part Two, time moves in measures of months and weeks. Each chapter in Part Two draws closer to decisive action until leaflet production begins.

## Suggestions for organizing reading circle interaction:

**1.**   As with Part One, the group may begin with another free association response to the concepts suggested by the chapter titles. Once again the discussion may move toward a focus on Germany, the Third Reich, WW2 and issues related to resistance.

**2.**   Group members may continue to each follow the evolution of specific individuals in the story, bringing that focus into the discussion. Also, auxiliary persons (such as Geyer, Grimminger, Eickemeyer and others brought to court in the second round of White Rose trials) are introduced in the narrative, providing more perspectives for individual discussion members to shadow. (These "associates" of the White Rose core may also become the subjects for individual spin-off research with later presentations that could enrich and amplify understanding of the on-going discovery of the White Rose story).

**3.**   Reading circle members might also choose a book, an author, a philosopher, an artist, a musician, a musical piece, or work of art that is mentioned as material that interested or influenced the development of White Rose members or the group in general. Fleshing out these points of interest could lead to a discussion of art as a form of resistance.

Digressions for Part Two: Pathways for further independent research

Chapter 6 "Alliances": Bishop Galen's sermons against euthanasia; Symbolism of the white rose; Writers influencing Hans Scholl; Intellectuals "in hiding."

Chapter 7 "Resolutions": Operation Barbarossa; Babi Yar; Einsatzgruppen; Universities and National Socialism.

Chapter 8 "Convergence": Schwabing; Sippenhaft; Military organization of the Student Companies.

Chapter 9 "Conscience": University life for women; Penalties for not reporting "subversive activities" to the authorities; Munich as the birthplace of Hitler's rise to power.

Chapter 10 "Departures": Atrocities in the occupied territories; Mass deportation of the Jews to labor and death camps; The Warsaw Ghetto.

Chapter 11 "Brutality": Conditions on the Russian front; Treatment of forced laborers.

Part Three consists of Chapters 12–18. The narrative spirals outward mirroring both the scope and the pace of the group's activity as it seeks to recruit members, gather funds and resources needed for the protest campaign, and to establish connection with other German resistance groups. Five of the seven chapters span a period of three months which brings the narrative into 1943 to the scene of Hans and Sophie's arrest as previously described in the Overture: Munich 1943. Chapter titles reflect this progression: Resistance, Circulation, Writing on the Wall, For Freedom, A Higher Court, Convictions, and To Life.

## Suggestions for organizing reading circle interaction:

1.   Begin again with the group or individuals responding to the chapter titles in a free association manner, gathering thoughts related to the concept in general and then bringing

concentration into the context of Germany, the Third Reich, and WW2, extending beyond as so inclined.

2. Group members may continue to shadow a particular individual throughout this section and to identify the places to which that individual traveled in efforts to "spread the word." (These "travels" may also become the basis for graphic representations of maps of the cities with White Rose contacts. Again these visuals could enrich and orient an understanding of the debate concerning methods and means as the White Rose reached out to other pockets of resistance).

**Digressions for Part Three: Pathways for further independent research**

**Chapter 12 "Resistance":** Other resistance efforts within Germany such as the "Red Orchestra."

**Chapter 13 "Circulation":** The Bonhoeffer group.

**Chapter 14 "The Writing on the Wall":** German defeat at Stalingrad; Definitions of treason.

**Chapter 15 "For Freedom":** No digression.

**Chapter 16 "A Higher Court":** The People's Court, Judge Roland Freisler.

**Chapter 17 "Convictions":** No digression.

**Chapter 18 "To Life":** Operation Zitadelle.

**Prologue and Epilogue**, the narrative's "Bookends." These bookends represent the author's memoir of two days in August, 2003, sixty years after the passing of the White Rose. Four American teachers travel to Crailsheim and Munich, Germany to visit schools named for and honoring members of the White Rose. They meet with German teachers in a discourse concerning the legacy of the White Rose and its implications in their work of educating young people, both in Germany and in the United States of America.

1. A group response to these accounts might revolve around themes that emerge throughout the *Journey to the White Rose in Germany*: youths' search for identity, influence of elders, evolution of personal conscience, and moral protest against the coer-

cion exercised by an absolute state whose abuse of basic human rights was rampant.

2.  Members of the reading circle may be encouraged to journal their own personal responses to the story represented in this book, allowing for private reflection with the option of later sharing these thoughts.

### A Study of the White Rose Leaflets and Leaflets of the Resistance.

Individual members of a reading circle could carry out a closer examination of a particular handbill and prepare to facilitate a discussion with the larger group.

As mentioned in this volume's **NOTES**, concept *summaries* of the leaflets' messages appear in the text in the following chapters: **Chapter 7**, the first leaflet summary; Chapter 9, the second, third and fourth leaflet summaries; **Chapter 13**, the fifth leaflet summary. **Chapter 14**, summary of Christoph Probst's draft; sixth leaflet summary.

Discussion participants may wish to read the actual texts or translations. The following website will lead to the appropriate sources:

<http://www.jlrweb.com/whiterose/html.>

**Key concepts** that form the basis of a discussion of the leaflets are as follows:
1.  checks and balances as a safeguard against corrupt leadership
2.  nationalism
3.  free will
4.  individuality and the common good
5.  political and spiritual awareness
6.  the relationship of law, power, and security
7.  social contract

8. civic virtue
9. deception for the sake of power
10. leadership or lack of leadership from intellectuals and the academic community
11. crimes against humanity
12. bystanders
13. family as primary social organization
14. Divine Order as a role model
15. government's respect or lack of for civil rights
16. passive resistance
17. government surveillance
18. democracy
19. world cooperation

CPSIA information can be obtained
at www.ICGtesting.com
Printed in the USA
FFOW02n1235280415
13000FF

9 781598 582490